Online Marketing Instruments and tactics for crafting online presence
-Case study included-

Daniel B. Smith

Daniel B. Smith Copyright © 2017

All rights reserved. No part of this publication may be reproduced, distributed or transmitted in any form or by any means, including photocopying, recording, or other electronic or mechanical methods, without the prior written permission of the author, excepting the case of brief quotations embodied in critical reviews and certain other noncommercial uses permitted by copyright law.

ONLINE MARKETING

Instruments and tactics for crafting online presence

-Case study included-

Table of contents

Introduction 4

Chapter I. The evolution of commerce and businesses 7

    I.1. Main phases and processes in the development of economy: from tribes to enterprises 7

    I.2. Customer behavior: new patterns and perspectives ... 15

    I.3. Transition from commerce to e-commerce 20

    I.4. Key e-commerce tactics for a nowadays company 29

Chapter II. The evolution of marketing theory and practices 33

    II.1. Phases in the evolution of marketing theory and practice 36

    II.2. Marketing mix-operational phase of the marketing process 41

    II.3. Online marketing–Concept, purpose and instruments 50

Chapter III. Implementing marketing instruments and tactics for promoting Sarcom Distribution Ltd. 58

    III.1. Short history of Sarcom Distribution Ltd. 58

    III.2. Marketing environment analysis 69

    III.3. Using online marketing instruments and tactics for promoting Sarcom Distribution Ltd. 84

Conclusion 110

References 113

Annexes 118

Conclusion 127

Introduction

The main purpose of my study is to present commerce evolution and marketing evolution-especially online marketing emergence-, along with its connections with other economics subdomains, all of these being necessary to be understood by every company which wants to perform in the actual economic environment. Thus, this study aims to identify at its end a set of online marketing specific actions which can be applied by every company so as to enhance organization performance and raise its value.

Research methods and procedures have helped me to reach the principal elements of this subject. After studying and analyzing each relevant aspect for my study, I have formed myself a general opinion on this subject.

My study is split in three chapters. In the first chapter I have identified some key historical steps which have made economy what it is today but especially the changes in economic relations and in the way of doing business. Another important element of the first chapter is represented by information and communications technology effects on economic actors and economic relations. All these elements have also modified customer behavior which is fairly important to be known by marketing specialist in order to achieve organization goals. I have presented the trend of electronic commerce evolution and I have analyzed a large range of elements which can assure organization success in this dynamic context. Thus, I have managed to identify some online action directions so as to achieve company success.

The second chapter focuses on the actual economic realities and marketing concept, its capabilities and online marketing emergence. The masterpiece of this chapter is the online marketing concept, a natural evolution of marketing, which offers for the professionals new instruments and tactics with which economic objectives can be reached easier. New technologies can be used by a wide range of entities, from the smallest firm, to the biggest company or public institutions. If they are used properly, the general result will always be the same: enhancing the organization.

In the final chapter of my study, I have presented my case study which is significantly based on my experience as a marketing specialist. I consider that is very useful for every company and organization to build their online presence and constantly optimize it. Through the analysis that I have made, I have found the most proper methods and instruments for doing that. I want to say once again that online marketing activity is characterized by a high degree of dynamism and requires permanent adjustments.

Finally, I have tried to formulate some clear conclusions which reveal the importance of using online marketing instruments and tactics. I am sure that my study can be further developed as new online marketing instruments, tactics and trends will appear. I strongly believe that this study is truly useful especially for small and medium companies, both nationally and internationally.

Chapter I. The evolution of commerce and businesses

I.1. Main phases and processes in the development of economy: from tribes to enterprises

A main characteristic of any organization is its internal organization, which is a management-related activity. The purpose of every economic agent is to gain profit and for achieving it, the company through its employees acts according to a business plan. Historically speaking, we can observe some similarities between a private organization and a tribe, which is extraordinary interesting.

The land has established a social relation: owners-workers. Slavery is historically traceable even in distant historical sources[1] and it was a reality which marked a lot of people and cultures. Depending on different law systems, slavery relations were a little bit different but the principle was the same.

Next stage is represented by feudalism. Feudalism is a system within which a social class-aristocrats- controls property rights of resources, including humans who are viewed as production factors. People who were part of an administrative unit were obliged to serve the

---
[1] Code of Hammurabi, 1750 B.C.

aristocrats: they either worked or fought, depending on needs. This form of organization is specific to middle ages.

"Commerce is an economic activity which refers to the exchange of goods, services or something of value, via sell-buy process"[2]. Generally speaking, the commerce doesn't refer just to goods or services, but anything that has a value for a person who may pay for obtaining it. The need for trade appeared when people started communicating with each other. One important idea is that people needs weren't always the same: time passing has modified them. For a well-known reference, let's consider Maslow's pyramid as being relevant for human needs. But it isn't always about human needs; nowadays is rather about human wants.

In the beginning, exchanges were conducted via barter[3]. For an exchange to happen, both parts had to have clear needs and to find an equilibrium value to evaluate their goods. This process was facilitated when currency started to be used[4]. From economics point of view, that is a historic moment because starting from that point we began to talk about seller, buyer and commerce implicitly[5].

---

[2] Investopedia, *Commerce*, available at http://www.investopedia.com/terms/c/commerce.asp, accessed on 1 December 2016.
[3] For instance, suppose a cow worthed twenty hens and four pigs.
[4] Filip, Pațac, *Istoria comerțului și turismului*, Editura Eurostampa, Timișoara, 2008, p.16.
[5] Albert, Rapin, *Cours de commerce*, Editura Dunod, Paris, 1983, p. 11-

Currency importance is more evident as we think about its functions. Thus, the currency guarantees free will if you were to choose a product or service and it also establishes a common measurement unit for goods and services. Actually, currency has enabled us to evaluate anything using the same unit, making thus all things easier to be compared.

As time went on, currency based exchanges took the place of barter which is barely used nowadays.

The currency has also created another opportunity: it allowed people to make money using money: thus, first banks appeared. "The history of banking activity can be traced back to ancient times, when Mesopotamian and Babylonian merchants offered credits for farmers and nearby traders"[6].

Mercantilism is a politic and economic paradigm which is characteristic to Europe, within period 1600-1800[7]. Mercantilism is a set of politic and economic actions which try to ensure economic and politic supremacy of a nation which is in competition with others.

12.
[6] Liviu, Guțuleac, *Cum au apărut primele bănci? Ce funcții îndeplineau? Ce tipuri de servicii ofereau?*, available at http://bancamea.md/news/cum-au-aparut-primele-banci-ce-functii-indeplineau-ce-tipuri-de-servicii-ofereau, accessed on 1 December 2016.
[7] Jean-Baptiste Colbert, prime minister between 1661 and 1683-during Louis XIV reign- was an exponent of economic regulations and mercantilism was a proper way to reach economic goals.

According to this system, the state had a central role in economy and its purpose was to amass rare metals-especially gold- via massive exports and minimum imports, generating thus a positive economic balance.

The end of eighteen century and the beginning of nineteen century is the period marked by the Industrial Revolution. Great technical discoveries[8] catalyzed impressive progresses and the switch from manufacture to mechanical processes happened. The first industry to benefit from that was British textile industry. Since that moment, the role of human within production process has constantly been changing: for instance, nowadays we talk about engineers, quality control employees, workers, economists, psychologists and so forth within a big producer. What we can easily observe even today is the technological gap between developed countries, under-development countries and so-called third world countries. Before the Industrial Revolution, there weren't so many differences between nations and productions processes. The Industrial Revolution, which originated in Europe, has also been used in a political way: superior military techniques and capabilities, steam engine propelled warships, power and resources desires, are just some aspects which catalyzed

---

[8] We cannot talk about Industrial Revolution without mentioning James Watt steam engine.

modern imperialism modern[9]. The most important effects of the Industrial Revolution[10] may be the following:
- Laissez-faire encouragement;
- Big companies emergence via businessmen money and property amass;
- New social structure-capitalism specific- emergence: rulers, church, army and police, aristocrats and common people;
- Urbanization: people from rural areas started to move into cities so as to gain more money;
- Social roles changes: women, children and men worked in order to earn money;
- Transportation network and means were improved;
- Historical law changes (Factories Regulations Act of 1833[11] and Outlawing the slavery in all British colonies in 1884);

---

[9] Michael C., Jensen, *The modern industrial revolution, exit, and the failure of internal control systems*, The journal of Finance, Vol. XLVIII, No.3, 1993.
[10] Christine, Golden, *Effects of the Industrial Revolution*, available at https://www.youtube.com/watch?v=0c0I62h-5g4, accessed on 2 December 2016.
[11] This act was available for England. It prohibited children under 9 from being employed in textile mills and limited the working hours of children under 18. It was a result of the Michael Sadler's report.

- Global commerce roots are established: products, services, capital and information.

Mercantilism decline is somehow marked by Adam Smith's work entitled "Nations' Wealth" among other factors which are related to context. I have to mention here both Karl Marx and Frederick Engels, who wrote about and conceptualized socialism. History shows that many states applied socialism at a point in their national existence whereas others applied capitalism; at the moment capitalism works better but there might come a moment when even this paradigm should fail. If you think about People's Republic of China, keep in mind that this country is a special one. When we talk about capitalism and socialism, we should realize that each paradigm comes with its own politic, economic and social features. Here are some fundamental ideas of capitalism[12]:
- Two main social classes: capitalism class and worker class. Labor division is a feature and the working class can invest in self specialization, resulting thus an intermediate social class;
- Companies exist to make profit, not only to satisfy customers' needs;
- Private property;

---

[12] Bruce R., Scott, *The political economy of capitalism*, Harvard Business School publications, 2006.

- Carelessness with regard to social equity;
- Minimum state intervention in economy;
- Profit is seen as an innovation catalyzer;
- Competitive market;
- High degree of adaptability to technological changes.

Here are some main ideas about socialism, so as to see more clearly the differences between these two economic systems[13]:

- Production means are public property;
- Public property and planning provide more just distribution of goods and services;
- Worker's value results from his time spent working, instead of final product's value;
- Great interest with regard to social justness and helping the poor;
- Individuals are dependent on state for all life aspects;
- Product's price is state-determined.

The most recent event which influences economic relations globally is the Information Revolution. When we refer to Industrial

---

[13] Wiliam James, Ghent, *The elements of socialism*, The new appeal publisher, Kansas, 1916.

Revolution things are fairly identified and scientists have formulated firm conclusions with regard to its impact on humankind. When it comes to Information Revolution, things are underway so it's very hard to identify all consequences and what is going to be next, especially because of the fast pace world is changing. Information Revolution effects are more or less visible. The concept of Information Revolution[14] has in its very core two factors: technology and information. Generally, the following are considered to be the main effects of Information Revolution:

- Technological progress and Internet emergence enable people to interact with each other, live, regardless distance;
- Information producing and transmitting costs have decreased;
- Possibility of finding creative solutions to societies' contemporary problems;
- Anybody can access human knowledge via Internet;
- New huge education opportunities: online books, online courses, online tutorials and so forth;
- It allows efficient goods and services allocation;

---

[14] Robert D. Atkinson and Andrew S. McKay, *Digital prosperity: Understanding the economic benefits of the information technology revolution*, I.T.I.F., Washington, 2007.

- New business opportunities and instruments to enhance organization value;
- Changes in business conducting and processes optimization have emerged: concepts like teleworking[15] and outsourcing[16] have appeared and have been implemented.

I.2. Customer behavior: new patterns and perspectives

An affirmation, an event or a symbol represents something else for any of us. We are unique and therefore we act differently. Psychologically speaking, patterns of justifying and foreseeing human behavior have been developed, which is useful for a lot of specialists from different fields of activity. Marketing specialists have realized that they can use knowledge of psychology and sociology[17] so as to identify patterns in customer behavior and thus influence them to a lesser or greater extent.

The main purpose of this subchapter is to identify-from marketing specialist's point of

---

[15] This concept defines using computers and other modern technical means so as to work from home.
[16] This concept defines certain processes externalization from a company to another which can fulfill them more cost efficiently.
[17] Interdisciplinary analysis is characteristic to nowadays scientific works and enables authors to connect information.

view- the context and conditions which influence customer buying decision.

Customer behavior has been studied by numerous scientists in order to explain and describe its mechanisms. Their work has led to establishing some fundamental ways of customer's behavior study[18]. These different ways represent distinct patterns of analyzing the same big theme, customer behavior and they also try to predict to some extent future actions.

It is necessary for any marketing specialist that he should know which factors influence customer behavior. It is useful to have at least some ideas with regard to this theme because through specific techniques, marketing specialist can sway potential customer's decisions. So as to understand the factors which influence to a greater or lesser extent customer behavior, we firstly have to see how a customer acts within purchasing process. Marketing specialists define purchasing process as being a mix of previous and further acquisition actions[19].

Usually, the purchasing process contains five phases[20]:

1. Problem or need identification;

---

[18] Marshallian framework, Pavlovian framework, Freudian framework, Veblenian framework and Hobbesian framework.
[19] Rodica, Boier, *Comportamentul consumatorului*, Editura Graphix, Iași, 1994.
[20] Daniela Morariu, Diana Pizmaș, *Comportamentul consumatorului: dileme, realități, perspective*, Editura Bibliofor, Deva, 2001.

2. Information gathering and analysis: In this stage, the customer uses all available information sources-Internet, recommendations, own experiences- so as to make the best choice. During this phase, spent time may be fairly big; informative articles found on specialty sites or blogs are important information resources for the customer. This is why it is recommended that every online marketing functional strategy should contain actions of educative/informative content generation. Further aspects with regard to this will be presented in this study;
3. Alternatives evaluation: In this phase, the customer seeks the best choice, based on previously gathered information. He uses general filters like price, quality, guarantee policy, brand but also specific filters depending on every customer;
4. Purchasing decision: At this moment, the customer has a lot of information so as to choose the right product. Generally, purchasing decision may be: a logical decision, an emotional decision or a decision influenced by marketing campaign. However, customer's decision cannot be entirely fit in one of these three patterns; it is rather a mix;

5. Post-sale evaluation: This phase is vital both for the customer and the organization. It is known that the product should rise to customer's expectations which were previously shaped whereby marketing activities. If the customer received a product which satisfies his expectations, he might become a brand ambassador, recommending thus the product to all his acquaintances. Marketing specialists are aware about the big value of world of mouth advertising. Marketing campaigns have to be carefully conceived and implemented because if the customer's expectations were high and the product didn't fulfill them, he would provide negative feedback with regard to the product and also the organization. Marketing specialists should not forget that contemporary means of communications enable a higher degree of transparency and provide easier access to information.

Within purchasing process, the customer is influenced by endogenous-internal- and exogenous-external- factors.

Endogenous influences are split in two main categories: psychological and personal. Psychological features like motivation, sensations, perceptions, representations,

language, memory, imagination, creativity, affection and attitude have been intensely studied by psychologists. All these psychological features influence people lives to the minutest details, from morning coffee to professional desires, from chosen clothes color to perfumes which make one feel comfortable. The second category of endogenous influences[21], personal factors, is represented by factors like:
- Demographic factors: age, sex, marital status, education level, work status, abode;
- Economic factors: personal income, abode income, price level, minimum wage level, inflation rate, shopping cart cost and so froth;
- Life style: It is the way an individual spends his time and money. The life style is constantly changing depending on individual's experiences and surrounding context.

Exogenous influences are also split in two main categories which influence customer behavior: family and cultural context.

---

[21] J.F. Engel and R.D. Blackwell, *Consumer Behavior*, The Dryden Press, Chicago, 1982.

I.3. Transition from commerce to e-commerce

In order to better understand commerce, we have to realize that nowadays society is like an immense interconnected spider web, where economic domain blends together with politic and social domain.

Through commerce, we understand any exchange of goods which is conducted through sell and buy process. From society sustainable development concept point of view, commerce is a strategic activity which assures society development and international relations creation through foreign commerce activities. In this context of socio-economic development, the merchant has a special role: he is the intermediary between production and consumption[22]. Commerce development is marked by some important phases[23]:

1. Preindustrial specific commerce: This period is mainly characterized by manufacture and penury. Craftsmen didn't produce a lot of goods and therefore demand could not be fully satisfied. Thus, goods were rapidly sold and merchant's role consisted in finding ideal areas to make business so as to

---

[22] This position offers attention from producers, consumers and politicians.
[23] Camelia, Băeșu, *Economia comerțului –Note de curs-*, Universitatea „Stefan cel Mare", Suceava, 2012, p.5.

maximize profits and make the most out of his goods.
2. Industrial revolution specific commerce: Historically speaking, Industrial Revolution is characteristic to a period somewhere between seventeen and nineteen century. New inventions changed people's life style but the biggest impact was on production means and processes.
3. Consumption economy specific commerce: Specialists consider that this type of commerce began approximately in 1950s and in underway. Mass production is a feature of this type of commerce and penury has been slowly replaced by fierce competition between different producers and distributors.

Internet appearance and spreading has led to evolution within many domains, from military domain to economy domain. It is sure that Internet makes our lives better, facilitates information access and has the power to bring us together. The most important Internet function is represented by easier and wider information access.

As regard electronic commerce concept, there are a lot of studies and specialty books which offer a large range of definitions. According to an online brochure of World Trade Organization, e-commerce is "the sale or purchase of good or services conducted over computer networks by methods specifically designed for the purpose of receiving or placing orders"[24]. This definition is somehow limitative because I have previously presented how a potential customer uses Internet during information gathering phase. Therefore, for my study, a wider definition which includes information importance during economic processes is proper. This definition is provided by Vladimir Zwass. According to the editor-in-chief of International Journal of Electronic Commerce, Vladimir Zwass, "Electronic commerce is sharing business information, maintaining business relationships and conducting business transactions by means of telecommunications networks"[25].

In order to present the opportunities provided by electronic commerce and better understand this concept, I consider that a comparative look between traditional commerce main characteristics and electronic commerce main characteristics is preferred[26]:
- *Traditional commerce:*

---

[24] World Trade Organization, *E-commerce in developing countries: opportunities and challenges for small and medium-sized enterprises*, Online Brochure, Switzerland, 2013.
[25] Vladimir, Zwass, *Electronic Commerce: Structures and Issues*, available at http://www.ijec-web.org/v1n1/p003full.html, accessed on 18 December 2016.
[26] Tutorialspoint, *E-commerce: electronic commerce approach*, Tutorials Point Online Brochure, India, 2014.

- It is based on direct interaction (face-to-face) and/or using landline phones and/or postal systems to exchange information;
- Transactions are manually processed;
- There is not a uniform platform of information providing because traditional commerce is based on interpersonal communication and therefore information distribution is difficult and uneven;
- The individual is involved in all business aspects.
- *Electronic commerce:*
  - It is based on indirect interaction via Internet and other communication technologies for information exchange;
  - Transactions are automatically processed;
  - There is a uniform platform for information providing. Through a website information can be offered in a customer-customized manner and information distribution can also be done easier;
  - The individual is involved in all business aspects.

The most important difference between these two ways of conducting business consists in the way information is transferred between business parties and processing methods. I want to assert once more that information has gained a central role in doing business.

Globally, electronic commerce is rising and this trend is highlighted by a lot of statistics presented by diverse publications. Electronic commerce transactions value differs according to each continent, North America being the leader when it comes to e-commerce[27]. Globally, in 2010, one third of Earth population was connected to Internet[28] and 30 people out of 100 were constant Internet users.

Globally, e-commerce market and Internet penetration level are rising; related information is available for Romania too. As regards electronic commerce, Romanian e-market is rising. E-commerce incomes for both goods and services worthed 77 million euros in 2006 and they have been rising since then; in 2016
e-commerce incomes totalized approximately 1,345 billion euros[29]. There is also an upward trend when it comes to Romanian Internet users[30], which strengthens online potential for any organization.

Before taking the decision of implementing online marketing functional

---

[27] See annex number 1.
[28] See annex number 2.
[29] See annex number 3.
[30] See annex number 4.

strategy, a marketing specialist makes a context analysis and searches for information in multiple sources in order to reach some pertinent conclusions. On the whole, no matter of field of activity or organization type, there are advantages and disadvantages of electronic commerce. Thus, the following may be considered as advantages of electronic commerce for an organization:

- By using electronic commerce, especially websites and communication capabilities provided by e-mail services, organizations can expand on regional, national and even global level;
- Information creation, processing and distribution costs may be reduced;
- Extended possibilities of information gathering, information which can be analyzed so as to optimize online marketing activities;
- Extended information distribution capabilities through Internet tools: social media, websites, news feeds.
- Enhancing organization brand;
- The possibility of providing more efficient assistance services for customers;
- Improving business processes-for instance supply activities, accounting activities- and even interconnecting them;

- Rising organization productivity.

From potential customer's point of view, by using electronic commerce, numerous advantages can be obtained. The most important advantage is that information is available 24/7 on Internet. Thus, it can be used anytime, without prior requesting: in my opinion this is also a strong point of nowadays functional online marketing strategies. The potential customer can obtain details about product technical specification, place orders and even pay them via online banking. Online information availability facilitates product comparison and purchasing decision is thus easier to be made. By using e-commerce, feedback providing is also encouraged because customers can easily post their post-sale impressions and experiences. It is easier for them to express their opinions about products and their opinions have a greater impact because they can be seen by potential customers or people who search for information about that specific product.

Electronic commerce offers advantages from societal point of view too. Potential customers didn't need to travel anymore so as to buy a certain product which is available only in a certain region; thus costs are reduced. Electronic commerce capabilities have also provided for rural communities the possibility of accessing products, services and information faster.

As regard electronic commerce disadvantages, the main issue is with regard to cyber security and personal data protection. There are also some integration incompatibilities between software and hardware components on one hand, and between different specific software on the other hand. A big drawback which has been solved recently was the big cost of creating, administering and optimizing a website. Online marketing specialists can nowadays use a wide range of instruments and tactics so as to reach organization goals and complex knowledge of programming or web design is not necessary, which is a great deal. A lot of platforms which are easy to use so as to create a website have appeared and costs are fairly small.

From customer's point of view, electronic commerce has some disadvantages like the lack of trust in online sellers, especially when the buyer is a traditional one and prefers face-to-face interactions. Even in this case, the utility of company online presence is proven: the potential customer can use Internet to obtain information about a certain product and buy it from a local store-offline-, rather than online. There is a set of regulation available at European Union level which encourages electronic commerce and protects potential customers.

Online transactions security is also a principal reason why a certain reticence is still present in doing such transactions; buyers prefer to pay the product when they receive it-cash on delivery-.

Electronic commerce security risks[31] represent another aspect which needs to be considered by online marketing specialist in collaboration with IT specialists. Generally, IT specialists have identified the following risks: cybernetic attacks, virus infections, malware software-which can steal or damage information- infections, improper use of cyber systems and system flaws/errors.

Security solutions have evolved very much: companies which offer website crafting platforms-either we talk about e-commerce websites or general websites- also provide integrated security solutions which are usually included in total price. These companies have decided to do so because one needs specialty training in order to be able to create website security solutions. The best example is Weebly[32] platform which offers all tools one needs to create an astonishing website, perfectly adjustable for any organization, and all security

---

[31] Dave, Chaffey, *E-business and e-commerce management – Strategy, implementation and practice*, 4th Edition, Prentice Hall, Harlow, 2009, p.652.
[32] www.weebly.com

aspects are in their responsibility. I will present in detail this platform and its capabilities in my study because it is the one I have used so as to create online presence for Sarcom Distribution Ltd.

I.4. Key e-commerce tactics for a nowadays company

As time passes by, changes are unavoidable. They emerge in every life domain and they take place at a fast pace: just image what phones we had ten years ago. No matter we talk about economic or social domain, about a county or another, about o powerful state or a less powerful one, we have to realize that because of globalization-mainly, but not only- humankind is nowadays interrelated and global community has never been so interdependent. One of the factors which have led to present situation is for sure the Internet; information sharing rapidity and easiness, implicitly.

Society progress has catalyzed changes in all life domains and as an effect, changes in people behavior have emerged: they way we interact, the way we spend out free time and the way we share information, are among the most important changes. From economic perspective, customer behavior has also changed: information access has swayed potential buyer-seller "power balance".

All these evolutions have deeply marked economic relations and the way of doing business. Therefore, no matter we talk about a local store, a medium company or a multinational company, every economic agent has to take into consideration the environment and make the best out of nowadays instruments and tactics which can be used in order to reach organization goals-they can be different at the first glance but the final purpose is to obtain profit-.

There are companies which build and implement an online marketing functional strategy having the purpose of providing information about the company and its products or services, pieces of advice and technical details, all of these contributing to medium and long term organization consolidation and potential customer number growth.

There are companies which build and implement an online marketing functional strategy only for gathering information about their consumers or test the market and there are companies which use online capabilities for creating an e-commerce platform which needs to be promoted through online marketing instruments and tactics.

No matter organization purpose, online presence in nowadays context is beneficial and recommended, especially because online marketing instruments and tactics can be implemented to serve a wide range of objectives. Both private and public institutions use more and more frequently the Internet during their activity; thus, I consider that an organization cannot miss online opportunities. Therefore, companies which want to grow and further develop in the online environment and organizations which want to establish and maintain a connection with their audience have to:

- Create an official social media platform page-according to statistics, Facebook is the biggest social media platform, globally[33]-;
- Build a website.

These two main ways of action are the principal ones so as to build online presence for the organization, regardless its purpose in online environment-e.g. to inform potential customers, to gather information, to promote a product and so forth-. These two ways have specific instruments and tactics which can be adjusted to fit organization goals. Further, I will approach marketing specific aspects and I will analyze the best practices and ways to build, measure and optimize a website and a social

---

[33] See annex number 5.

media official page, according to online marketing best practices.

Chapter II. The evolution of marketing theory and practices

Marketing concept is an enormous one and there is no universal definition, either we talk about marketing specialists or theoreticians. Nowadays there are at least 72 definitions with regard to this concept[34]. Even if this concept is so intricate, there are some paradigms which are based on common elements. By using the marketing concept one can refer to a field of study, a science domain, or a practical activity, for instance a marketing campaign which aims to locally promote a product. Regardless of the chosen perspective to define this concept, we always find the importance of information as a base element, no matter its form.

The American Marketing Association Board of Directors defines marketing as: "the activity, set of institutions, and processes for creating, communicating, delivering, and exchanging offerings that have value for customers, clients, partners, and society at large"[35].

---

[34] Heidi Cohen, *72 Marketing Definitions*, available at http://heidicohen.com/marketing-definition/, accessed on 12 March 2017.
[35] American Marketing Association, *Definition of Marketing*, available at https://www.ama.org/AboutAMA/Pages/Definition-of-Marketing.aspx, accessed on 12 March 2017.

Philip Kotler says about marketing that: "is the science and art of exploring, creating, and delivering value to satisfy the needs of a target market at a profit"[36].

For my study and its objectives, the following definition by Julie Barile, Vice President of e-Commerce of Fairway Market is relevant: "Marketing is traditionally the means by which an organization communicates to, connects with, and engages its target audience to convey the value of and ultimately sell its products and services. However, since the emergence of digital media, in particular social media and technology innovations, it has increasingly become more about companies building deeper, more meaningful and lasting relationships with the people that they want to buy their products and services"[37].

Likewise different concepts have been improved during time passing, defining marketing concept has generated two paradigms which are specific for different time periods. These changes are natural, economic domain being characterized by dynamism, especially nowadays when globalization and information technology are great forces which

---

[36] Kotler Marketing Group, *What is Marketing?*, available at http://www.kotlermarketing.com/phil_questions.shtml#answer3, accessed on 12 March 2017.
[37] CNNiReport, *Smart Beautiful Digital Marketing ~ 10 Definitions of Marketing*, available at http://ireport.cnn.com/docs/DOC-1237333, accessed on 12 March 2017.

may influence to a lesser or greater extent everything.

These two big paradigms have influenced marketing practices and theoretical approaches[38]. The turning point is the middle of twenty century, century which is characterized by the two World Wars, Great Economic Crisis, totalitarian regimes, subtle politic games between U.S.A. and U.S.S.R. and other historical events. The first paradigm is peculiar to the first half of the twenty century: according to it, the core of marketing is represented by the products which needed to be sold. The second paradigm is specific to the second half of the twenty century: according to it, the core of marketing is represented by the customer. It also establishes connections with other domains of science.

The importance of marketing results from the advantages of applying it[39]. The advantages are diverse and incite actions to be taken if they are understood by decisional factors. Both public and private organizations may make use of marketing practices by using the tools provided by technological progress so as to fulfill organizational goals: for example, public

---

[38] Dr. Horia Mihai, Răboacă, *Curs de marketing*, available at http://www.apubb.ro/wp-content/uploads/2011/02/Marketing_suport_de_curs.pdf, accessed on 12 March 2017.
[39] Smriti, Chand, *7 Major Importance of Marketing*, available at http://www.yourarticlelibrary.com/marketing/7-major-importance-of-marketing-marketing-management/25857/, accessed on 12 March 2017.

campaigns for informative purposes with regard to alcohol consumption or recruitment campaigns undertaken via online marketing means. I consider that presenting some advantages which may be obtained through marketing practices is the best solution to provide the big picture view of opportunities like:
- Establishing a relation between organization and customer;
- Providing support for decision making via provided information;
- Improving organization's brand and image;
- Enhancing products, rising creativity and facilitating sales;
- Helping to position inside market and providing means to test which marketing practices work better for ensuring organization success.

II.1. Phases in the evolution of marketing theory and practice

When we talk about marketing history and evolution it is necessary to make a distinction between marketing ideas and practices and marketing as a field of study. The marketing ideas and practices are bound to commerce history: it's obvious that antique merchants promoted their products and knew their customers. On the other side, the marketing as a field of study has its origin somewhere between nineteen century and twenty century[40].

Within specialty literature, there are two well-known authors-Robert Bartels[41] and Philip Kotler[42]- who designed two widely-spread schemes which present marketing evolution.

Robert Bartels considers marketing evolution as having its point of origin in the beginning of twenty century[43]:

- **Discovery period (1900-1910):** It is the moment when marketing was fixed as a different field of study. Up to this point, marketing had been based on studying its rules and best practices coming from economic agents, with regard to distribution and products sales process. It is also the phase when first studies and works on marketing were elaborated.
- **Concept period (1910-1920):** It is the period when both concepts and marketing notions are defined, developed and classified.
- **Integration period (1920-1930):** Within this period marketing principles

---

[40] Dr. Horia Mihai, Răboacă, Op. Cit., p.11.
[41] Robert, Bartels, *The History of Marketing Though*, 2nd edition, Columbus (Ohio), 1988.
[42] Philip, Kotler, *Marketing Management*, 11th edition, Prentice Hall, New York, 2001.
[43] Jagdish N. Sheth, David M. Gardner, *History of Marketing Thought: An Update*, University of Illinois, 1982, p. 2.

were defined-consumption maximization, customer satisfaction maximization, portofolio enlargement and life quality maximization[44]- and a series of knowledge, methods and approaches from other fields of study were integrated, like math and sociology. During this interval, marketing started to be split into subdomains like advertisement, sales and distribution.

- **Development period (1930-1940):** Marketing domain and its subdomains started to develop; marketing-related hypotheses were validated or invalidated. In U.S.A. marketing magazines and journals started to be published for professionals and specialists.
- **Re-evaluation period (1940-1950):** Traditional knowledge started to be considered again. New marketing approaches were developed: marketing management[45] and marketing as a system[46].

---

[44] Lectiieconomice.net, *Principiile Marketingului*, available at http://www.lectiieconomice.net/marketing/concept/28-principiile-marketingului.html, accessed on 7 April 2017.
[45] It represents the organizational discipline which focuses on the practical application of marketing orientation, techniques and methods inside enterprises and organizations and on the management of a firm's marketing resources and activities.
[46] When one talks about marketing as a system, he refers to a network

- **Reconceptualization period (1950-1960):** It is the period when new approaches appeared, which aimed both managerial processes and marketing social implications. Tools like marketing analyses and quantitative researches- like questionnaire- were increasingly applied. Concepts with strong sociology links were developed: organizational behavior and customer behavior.
- **Differentiation period (1960-1970):** It is the period when the focus was shifted on marketing management, customer behavior and marketing system. Quantitative analyses and researches became popular and the information acquired through this way was appreciated.
- **Socialization period (1970-present):** This period is marked by a paradigm shift. How marketing may influence the society is the new question and not how society may influence marketing.

Philip Kotler proposes a more concise scheme to highlight marketing evolution[47]:
- **Product orientation:** 1900-1920
- **Sales orientation:** 1920-1950

---

of buyers, sellers and other actors that come together to trade in a given product or service.
[47] Philip, Kotler, *Managementul marketingului: Analiza, Planificare, Implementare, Control,* Teora Publisher, Bucharest, 1999.

- **Marketing orientation:** 1950-1970
- **Social marketing orientation:** 1970-prezent

Authors like Daniel Pope, John Goodman, Roger Kerin and others have developed own schemes with regard to marketing evolution but for my study the above-presented are enough.

Nowadays, technological, economic and social progress together with increasing competition, represent fundamental premises in each marketing activity. Thus, no matter what tools one uses to highlight marketing environment, these aspects are there and need to be taken into consideration.

Both organizations and professionals have realized how important it is to put emphasis on potential customer when tackling marketing, to inform him and to obtain information about him. Therefore, production and sales are not anymore the main focus, but customer satisfaction. In this new environment, organizations are forced to select proper methods and means of marketing in order to achieve their goals. The novelty in marketing evolution-mainly catalyzed by technological progress- is represented by online marketing, which offers a new perspective of carrying marketing activities along with advantages, as I will further present.

II.2. Marketing mix-operational phase of the marketing process

Nowadays, most markets are characterized by intense competition. In this context, an organization cannot afford to act randomly or only by rule of thumb- this approach to doing business may be peculiar to small and medium companies which usually don't have a vision on short or medium term- but more efforts need to be made. A wider view is needed so as to gather information, to analyze it and to generate a coherent direction of development.

From marketing point of view, the organization has to identify a way of discovering customer's needs and penetrate the market with products crafted taking into consideration customer's needs and wants. Thus, marketing process is the way through which the company prospects the market, establishes directions of action, decides with regard to marketing mix, implements and controls decisions. Therefore, the marketing process is composed of actions on the following directions[48]:

- Situational analysis (market research);

---

[48] NetMBA Business Knowledge Center, *The Marketing Process*, available at http://www.netmba.com/marketing/process/, accessed on 8 April 2017.

- Strategic level: mass marketing or target marketing (segmentation, targeting, positioning and value proposition);
- Operational level: marketing mix (product, price, placement and promotion);
- Implementation and control.

The situational analysis represents the first phase within marketing process because the organization has to focus on itself firstly so as to identify internal and external factors which may represent capabilities, vulnerabilities, opportunities and threats. It is important that the organization should know these aspects in detail because they represent the base for further marketing actions.

There are several frameworks which can be used for information gathering: 5C Analysis[49], PEST analysis[50]-it can be used as climate analysis tool within 5C analysis- and SWOT analysis[51]. When analyzing, the marketer should also take into consideration market specific variables like: market dimension and market dynamics.

On the whole, a situational analysis includes past, present and future company aspects, highlighting events which have

---

[49] Company, Customers, Competitors, Collaborators and Climate.
[50] Aims to clarify macro-environment factors: Political, Economic, Social and Technological.
[51] Strengths, Weaknesses, Opportunities and Threats.

influenced the organization: a competitor, a partnership, new ways of promotion, a crisis, new technological means and so forth.

When the analysis result shows a big difference between customer's wants and what the market can offer for him, the firm may introduce in the market better products. However, the decision must take into consideration customer behavior trends, product type, research and development costs and other highly-volatile elements.

The strategic level is composed of actions based on the situational analysis, with regard to: segmentation, targeting, positioning and value proposition. According to context, the organization may choose mass marketing- treating the market as a homogeneous group and offering the same marketing mix- or target marketing.

The concept of target marketing recognizes customers' diversity and does not try to satisfy all customers with the same offer. Target marketing includes three activities: market segmentation, market targeting and market positioning. If the organization decides to use target marketing, it must clearly define which segments will be capitalized on. The segments must have the following features in order to be useful: "be measurable, be substantial, be accessible, be differentiable and be actionable"[52]. The segmentation process may be done based on features like: geographical factors, demographical factors, psychological factors or a mix between them, according to company's needs.

Targeting activity is based on segment attractiveness; for analyzing it, elements like the following are considered: segment size, competition, customer loyalty, rise potential, advertisement capabilities, sales potential and forecasted profit.

Positioning within target segment is based on spreading information which shows the advantages of using certain products or services towards potential customers.

Value proposition is a marketing or business statement that a company uses to express why a potential consumer should buy a product or use a service. Thus, it's what the consumer can obtain only from that specific company.

Operational level is represented by marketing mix concept. The concept became well-known after Neil H. Borden published an article entitled *The Concept of the Marketing Mix*, in 1964. The concept describes the perfect combination of four elements, according to company context, in order to reach company goals. Generally speaking, through marketing mix, one refers to four dimensions around

---

[52] Philip Kotler, Kevin Lane Keller, *Marketing Management*, 14th Edition, Prentice Hall Publisher, 2012, p. 231-232.

which marketing activity focuses: product, price, placement and promotion[53]. This number may be extended, depending on organization type and what factors it considers to be relevant. The following may be part of marketing mix: people, brand, conditions, shelf exposure, complementary services, logistics, information and so forth.

The product represents any thing which can be sold to satisfy a need or want: goods and services, experience, events, people, places, firms, ideas and information. In order to address demand-effective and potential-, the marketing specialist analyses all product attributes-quality, design, characteristics, brand, package, dimensions, warranty- because these are what customers value. There is also a new concept named "total product" which refers to the totality of additional benefits one receives when buying a product; for instance, extended free warranty for 1 year. A very significant aspect which needs to be considered when talking about product policy is the brand. The brand, if used properly, may fulfill functions like[54]:

- Confirming product originality;
- Stimulating demand for the product-as compared to an unbranded one-;

---

[53] Academia Navala "Mircea cel Batran", *Marketing: Note de curs*, Constanta, 2008, p.136.
[54] Gheorghe Băşanu, Dumitru Fundătură, *Management şi Marketing*, Diacon Coresi Publisher, Bucharest, 1993, p. 180-181.

- Differentiating the product;
- Stimulating quality improvement.

From the four elements which constitute the marketing mix, the price is the only one which ensures revenues whereas others are considered expenses. Among others, price policy is the most adaptable: it may be quickly adjusted whereas product policy, placement policy and promotion policy require more time for adjustments. The price may be view from two perspectives: for customers it represents the cost for satisfying a need or want; for companies it represents the main revenues source. Philip Kotler has elaborated a six-step procedure for establishing the price policy. However, I have to mention that small and medium companies do not make such analyses; they rather charge industry specific margins. Philip Kotler's framework with regard to the price policy is the following[55]:

1. Selecting the pricing objective
2. Determining demand
3. Estimating costs
4. Analyzing competitors' costs, prices and offers
5. Selecting a pricing method
6. Selecting the final price.

Placement policy represents the way through which an organization decides to

---
[55] Philip Kotler, Kevin Lane Keller, Op. Cit., p. 389.

penetrate the market with its good and/or services. Generally, the placement concept may represent: the path on which good and services are delivered from the producer to the customer; the operations which are done during goods delivery like loading, handling, unloading, storing; technical and material means which are needed for placement operations. Both theoreticians and professionals consider that through placement policy the following are fulfilled: bringing the product closer to the final customer; establishing an informational link which works both ways and demand stimulation. In order to obtain an efficient placement policy, the organization should analyze and project a distribution chain which ought to fulfill: physical goods distribution, information delivery and auxiliary distribution-related activities. Depending on organization type and its objectives, there are some types of different distribution networks.

The promotion policy is an important element of marketing mix. In the actual economic and social context, promotion may ensure organization success or failure. Through promotion we refer to certain activities and processes which aim to let people know about a new product, having the purpose of facilitating market penetration and sales stimulation. Everything may be promoted: goods, services, people, events, information and so forth.

Promotion is an activity which enables marketing specialist to use his creativity and intelligence by crafting a performant promotion policy. The promotion may have different objectives according to whom it addresses, specific tools being accordingly adjusted. No matter which instruments one uses for promotion, the focus should be on information providing via an optimal communication process because as I previously said, the information has a crucial role in buying decision. Therefore, so as to satisfy information demand, the organization has to build a communication system which ought to assure a permanent link with every potential customer.

Philip Kotler proposes a genuine vision of promotion policy, which he calls marketing communication mix, composed by major nodes of communication[56]:

- Advertising via print media, broadcast media, network media, electronic media and display media (offline-online);
- Sales promotion (offline-online);
- Events and experiences (mainly offline);
- Public relations and publicity (mainly offline);
- Direct marketing (mainly online);

---

[56] Philip Kotler, Kevin Lane Keller, Op. Cit., p.478.

- Interactive marketing (mainly online);
- Word-of-mouth marketing (mainly offline);
- Personal selling (face-to-face interaction, mainly offline).

The technological progress has catalyzed online marketing emergence and also made it harder to distinguish between offline and online environment. For instance, sales promotion may be done via offline instruments (banners posted in high traffic areas) or via online instruments (online banners).

From online marketing perspective, the company may mainly use:
- Website marketing
- Social media marketing
- Search engine marketing(Google Adwords, Google Keyword Planner)
- Content marketing
- Email marketing
- Affiliate marketing.

The final step of the marketing process is represented by marketing plan implementation and control. The business environment is more and more dynamic and this requires a continuous monitoring and adjusting of marketing practices. The good news is that adjustment possibilities are multiple and the promotion policy is the most frequently adjusted as compared to other marketing mix elements.

II.3. Online marketing–Concept, purpose and instruments

The technological progress has catalyzed changes in marketing theory and practices, adapting it to nowadays economic realities. New methods of engaging with customers have emerged and there is a whole new set of instruments which may be used to obtain information on potential customers, delivery information and enhance company image. Therefore, it is true to say that the Internet and new technologies have changed the seller-buyer interaction.

Online environment offers numerous benefits for marketing activities: it represents a new way of communication and reduces information delivery costs. Broadly, Internet advantages may transfer to online marketing advantages, being such a great opportunity for organizations.

Online marketing may be defined as the usage of Internet and other digital technologies so as to reach marketing objectives[57]. Philip Kotler considers online marketing as being "a form of marketing which connects the customer

---

[57] Webopedia, *Internet marketing*, available at http://www.webopedia.com/TERM/I/internet_marketing.html, accessed on 9 April 2017.

with the seller via technological instruments such as: e-mails, websites, online forums and newsgroups, interactive television, mobile communications etcetera"[58].

When it comes to online marketing, specialists talk about the concept of 10Cs, representing zones which require marketing specialist's attention to understand what drives online marketing[59]: Client, Corporative culture, Convenience, Competition, Communication, Consistency, Creative content, Customization, Coordination and Control.

As I have presented in Chapter I, the Internet has changed customer behavior: the main source of used by the potential customer for information gathering is nowadays the Internet. Therefore, online marketing specialist has to focus on satisfying customer's information needs. Different instruments are used according to the objectives of the marketing plan.

Online marketing scope is closely related to organization business model and marketing plan implicitly. Some companies may use online marketing tools just to promote their image in the online environment while others may open

---

[58] KnowledgeBrief, *Digital Marketing*, available at https://www.kbmanage.com/concept/digital-marketing, accessed on 9 April 2017.
[59] Richard Gay, Alan Charlesworth and Dr. Rita Esen, *m@rketing on-line: o abordare orientată spre client*, All Publisher, Bucharest, 2009, p.12.

an online store. In both situations online marketing instruments may be used for business optimization. For instance, if the purpose of marketing specialist were to revitalize a small company through crafting online presence, he would concentrate on website marketing and social media marketing. It is also possible that he would use search engine marketing, affiliate marketing and e-mail marketing but these instruments are not the best for this example.

Generally speaking, online marketing offers the following advantages of using its specific instruments:

- **Cost reduction:** promotion costs are significantly reduced, their efficiency being thus raised. Information processing costs are also reduced.
- **Enhanced capabilities:** Online marketing instruments provide new product and services development opportunities via new markets exploring.
- **Competitive advantage:** If a company reached Internet before its competitors and strengthens its position, it would certainly obtain a competitive advantage over its competitors. This advantage may be extended during time by implementing constant online promotions.

- **Enhanced communications:** The communication process is facilitated because the organization may be contacted 24/7 via e-mail or online forms.
- **Better control:** Online marketing instruments and tactics are at a click away. Thus, adjusting an online marketing campaign can rapidly be done and I also have to point out its flexibility.
- **More satisfied customers:** Either we talk about a customer who seeks information about the company or a certain product or we refer to a customer who places an online order, if online marketing instruments and tactics are correctly applied, the customer will encounter a positive user experience and will be more satisfied.
- **Multiple options:** Online marketing offers multiple options for reaching organization objectives. Thus, according to its objectives, the organization may choose to make use of: website marketing, search engine marketing, social media marketing, viral marketing, email marketing, affiliate marketing.

Website marketing represents the use of a company's website in order to reach certain marketing goals like getting as much traffic on it and convert this traffic into buyers, members or whatever the purpose of the site is. The website can be an e-commerce one or just an informative website. The website marketing concept focuses on the website and includes both technical aspects and specific tactics such as: website design, index rate, search engine optimization, content marketing, alt-text for photos, keywords embedded into website code and so forth. It is important that all this elements should be interconnected so as to reach a high website profile.

Frequently, an Internet user stars using web by accessing a search engine-Google, Yahoo Search, Bing and so forth-. A search engine is a program which searches into a database-this database is composed of the majority of websites, classified according to specific algorithms- for certain keywords which are typed by the user. Depending on which keywords the user uses and how the organization website is designed, the search engine classifies the search results and provides them to the user. Shortly, this is the process of information searching. Through search engine marketing, specialists can apply some measures to enhance company presence in the online environment. **Search engine marketing** has three forms of being applied[60]:

---

[60] Rafi, Mohammed, *Internet Marketing*, McGraw Hill, New York, 2004, p.408.

- Submitting the website to the search engine for registering and indexing it;
- Paid advertisement based on certain keywords, which will trigger the ad and deliver it among search results' first positions;
- Online banners.

Social media marketing represents that way through which the organization uses social networks-Facebook, YouTube, Twitter, LinkedIn, Instagram and others- so as to reach goals like: organization promotion, discount sales promotion, product promotion and so forth. Every organization has to realize the importance of social networks and their upward trend. If used properly, social media marketing would help in:
- "Generating exposure to businesses
- Increasing traffic/subscribers
- Building new business partnerships
- Raising among search engine rankings
- Generating qualified leads due to better lead generation efforts
- Selling more products and services
- Reducing marketing expenses."[61]

Another aspect which worth being mentioned with regard to social media

---

[61] Sisira, Neti, *Social media and its role in marketing*, International Journal of Enterprise Computing and Business Systems, Vol.1 Issue 2, Warangal, July 2011, p.6.

marketing is the concept of **viral marketing**, which represents a method of marketing whereby consumers are encouraged to share information about a company or its goods or services via the Internet.

Email marketing represents the usage of e-mails to reach marketing objectives. According to in force regulations, the most controversial aspect of this instrument is the well-know spam; this situation has been tackled by European Union UE through a Directive on communications and confidentiality[62], dating from 2002. The thing is that these e-mails are not randomly sent. There are companies which create e-mail databases and sell them. The information is gathered via online means, especially when the customer buys something via Internet, expressing thus his acceptance of terms and conditions which seldom are read. Therefore, an organization can buy an e-mail database according to specific criteria, so as to target certain people. Email marketing may be used for[63]: delivering short news, delivering new products information, announcing the availability of certain products, announcing discounts, confirming orders, delivering customized messages, ensuring technical help,

---

[62] Directive 2002/58/CE of European Parliament and European Union Council.
[63] Richard Gay, Alan Charlesworth and Dr. Rita Esen, *Op. Cit.*, p.404.

realizing questionnaires, delivering thank you messages and so forth.

Chapter III. Implementing marketing instruments and tactics for promoting Sarcom Distribution Ltd.

This chapter presents how I have implemented online marketing instruments and tactics so as to enhance Sarcom Distribution Ltd. awareness and improve overall business. Thus, I have presented the company, its marketing environment and all the actions I have taken for it, together with information analysis and recommendation formulation.

III.1. Short history of Sarcom Distribution Ltd.

Sarcom Distribution Ltd. was founded in 1992 and it commercializes chemical products. It's a small size company that doesn't exceed a turnover of 500.000 euros per year and it has two employees. The headquarters is located in Râmnicu Vâlcea town and this company is the official distributor of Sarcom Ltd.[64] for Vâlcea County. Therefore, the company activity focuses mainly on Vâlcea County.

Because of the seriousness with which the company treats each order, the compliance with

---

[64] This company is the producer of Sticky products, the plant being located in Vâlcea County. The company is in top 15 within paints and varnishes Romanian industry, among: Policolor, Dufa, Deutek, Kober, Sentosa Impex, Fabryo and Azur. Company website: www.sticky.ro

delivery terms for customers and the accent on the business relations, the company is fairly known locally. The company considers that the communication and negotiation processes are the main factor which has contributed to firm survival into fierce local competition, despite all business conducting encountered difficulties.

Product portofolio includes: alchidic paints, primers, alchidic varnishes, water-based varnishes, diluents, washable paints, adhesives, decorative paints, dyes and pigments, road marking paints and auxiliary products. During the production processes, Sarcom Ltd. puts emphasis on raw materials quality and production technologies, which ensures an unbeatable quality-price report for customer.

There are two brands which are sold by Sarcom Distribution Ltd.: Sticky and Coral. Sticky-branded products aim middle class people and are well-known locally, being thus considered the best choice by the customers: high quality, low price and easy to be used. Coral-branded products aim above middle class people and are premium quality: the producer uses the best raw materials and technological processes so as to craft these products and the brand is still under development. However, as compared to Sticky-branded product, they are more expensive but their price is still bellow competitors'. Coral products can easily compete on international market; locally, customers prefer Sticky products.

As the producer wanted to ensure its customers about its products' quality, Sarcom Ltd. has acquired ISO 9001 certification-Quality Management System-. Thus, the company and its products have acquired the following advantages:
- Enhanced organization image and production processes;
- Consolidated trust between business partners;
- Better customer satisfaction because of enhanced products;
- Internationally renowned quality standard;
- Compliance with auctions requirements.

Paints and varnishes industry constantly changes. This industry is influenced by a lot of factors like: regulations, V.A.T., raw materials' price, real estate investments and so forth. This industry is highly bound to real estate sector and varies accordingly. Paints and varnishes market recorded in 2015 an approximate value of 170 million euros[65] and in 2016 a value of

---

[65] Ziarul Financiar, *Piata de lacuri si vopsele decorative, in crestere pe fondul constructiilor rezidentiale noi*, available at http://www.zf.ro/constructii-imobiliare/piata-de-lacuri-si-vopsele-decorative-in-crestere-pe-fondul-constructiilor-rezidentiale-noi-15294091, accessed on 10 March 2017.

178.5 million euros. For 2017, estimations foresee a value of about 185 million euros. Sarcom Ltd.-the producer-had revenues of around 30 million Romanian lei in 2015, which places the company in top 15 companies in this industry, with first positions being held by Kober, Fabryo-Atlas and Azur.

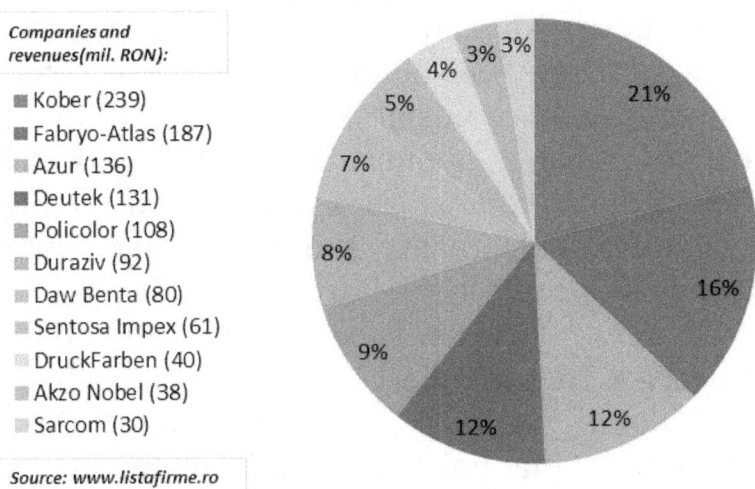

In these conditions-having a market share of approximately 3%-, Sarcom Ltd. ought to rethink its development strategy in order to rise its market share and a possible way to do it is represented by specific marketing activities. If the company undertook marketing activities like promotion, it would foster Sticky and Coral brands and also support local distributors in their efforts. However, for my study, the development of Sarcom Distribution Ltd.-Valcea county official distributor- is relevant.

I have already presented that Sarcom Distribution Ltd.[66] activates only within Valcea county-based on the contract which was signed with the producer-; it is a small size company both by its revenues and its employees.

Since 1992 up to now, Sarcom Distribution has been doing business into 2 ways, both adapted to different marketing context. There is a unanimously accepted opinion within businessmen groups: each economic change is more intense felt by small and medium companies as compared to big companies. This reality should be taken into consideration when at European and national levels new policies will be crafted. We should not forget that middle class is based on these small and medium companies and thus, economic public policies should be focused on helping these companies to develop.

First method of doing business is typical for period 1992-2013, which was a period with numerous economic challenges and a high level of uncertainty. These aspects are valid nationally speaking because the transition to a free market consolidated economy is still underway. Adjusting Romanian economy to European Union's and especially the impact on small and medium companies have deeply

---

[66] Website: www.vopselevalcea.com

marked Romanian business environment and capital. There are some gaps between Romania and so-called economic engines of European Union like Germany or France: education system, social system, healthcare system, entrepreneurial culture, security culture and so forth; all these gaps influence in a bigger or smaller degree each one's life: my point is that sooner or later we will all realize that we are globally interconnected. Another important characteristic of this period is the Romanian entrepreneurs' lack of business experience- taking into consideration our experience with communism and centralized economy- and high bureaucracy level. Coming back to the main idea, during this period, the company has been doing business according to the following scheme:

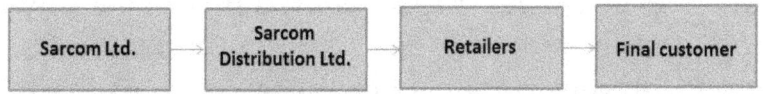

Figure 1: First Business Model of Sarcom Distribution Ltd.

The goods were acquired from the producer-which offered a discount between 10% and 17%- and sold to customers-retailers-. In this period, Sarcom Distribution's customers were only the retailers, which owned stores all over Valcea County and exhibited the products. Different discounts have been negotiated with the biggest retail companies, based on orders' value and their frequency. There were some business relations with public institutions but they were rather sporadic. This business model worked very well for Valcea county market, which was covered by small and medium retailers. With regard to this business scheme, low costs were for sure a strong point. The biggest disadvantage of this business model was that it took too much time for Sarcom Distribution to be paid by retailers for the goods: from thirty to ninety days since the moment of products delivery. Please keep in mind that this situation is locally generalized when it comes to business environment. The beginning of 2008 well-known crisis combined with competitors' local market penetration have considerably influenced both Sarcom Distribution's revenues and business partners'- some of them have gone bankrupt-. The main issue here is that those companies can't pay their liabilities and the products providers won't get the money back because the whole bankrupt businesses were going on bank loans. This is the situation of Sarcom Distribution which is supposed to get back from retailers some money but actually it won't see a penny. Therefore, the company has to cover this money from business operations and after a long period pay for the loss. Another crucial aspect was the penetration of local market by Dedeman and Ambient, two huge retailers, one of which has already downsized its business-

Ambient-. Thus, the company's priority with regard to the period 2009-2013, was to ensure survival and try to find new business partners.

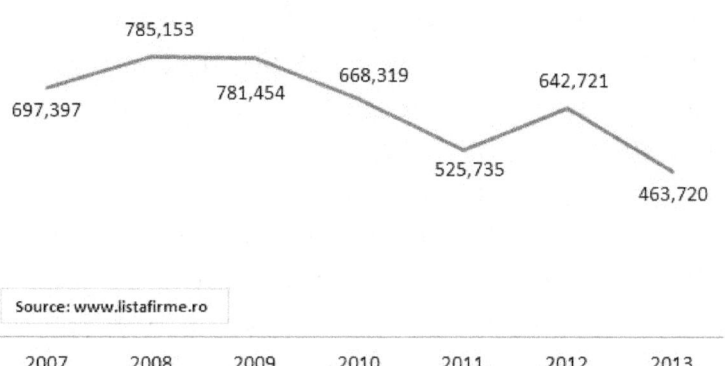

As you can easily observe, the revenue has been diminishing, reaching the period minimum in 2013. During the following years- 2014 and 2015-, the revenue was following a downward trend. That context urged finding a new way of doing business. At the end of 2013, we decided to make an analysis and see what the main issues of the business were. We identified two big problems: which negatively affected Sarcom Distribution Ltd.: 1. Retailers were having difficulties in selling the products and were losing clients in the advantage of big retailers like Dedeman and Ambient; 2. Competition on local market was growing, nationally known brands as Kober, Policolor, Dufa, Fabryo, Azur having penetrated the local market. The number of low cost substitutes was also rising. That was the sensitive context which fostered business model adjustment.

The second business model was implemented in 2014 and the company has been operating according to it since then. The sales continued to drop and additionally, the number of clients was dropping: business partners-retailers- were forced by economic conditions and/or poor management to close their operations or change the industry. Therefore, uncovered market zones appeared and there was a new opportunities for the players. This was the context within which the firm decided to build its own store in Râmnicu Vâlcea city, having the purpose of targeting potential customers who were living in town and a small radius- maximum 20 kilometers-. Nowadays the company runs respecting this business model, which looks as follows:

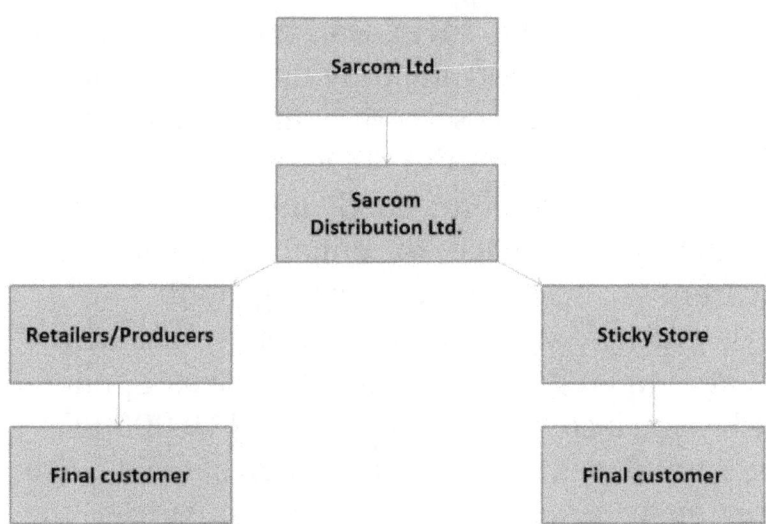

Figure 2: Second business model of Sarcom Distribution Ltd.

Starting with year 2014, the company respected the previously presented business model. Basically, our traditional business partners, either we talk about county retailers, plants or public institutions, are not affected-or if they should be, the level of influence is very low- by the opening of Sticky store in Râmnicu Vâlcea because it aims at serving customers who were living in town and a small radius- maximum 20 kilometers-.

Building this store was a strategic movement for Sarcom Distribution Ltd. and I consider that the following advantages were acquired: own display store, lower prices for final customer, possibility of providing specialty pieces of advice, enhancement of Sticky and Coral brands, bigger portofolio, cash on sale and last but not least, possibility of attracting new customers and revenues growth. These advantages will be valued by mixing traditional marketing practices with online marketing. Thus, this study has the objective of identifying the best instruments and tactics of online marketing in order to enhance Stick Store awareness and ensure company growth.

Sticky store construction took three months-in August 2014 the store was opened- and it had a cost of approximately 110.000 RON[67]- the capital was obtained from own savings-. As I previously said, despite store opening, the downward trend remained in 2014 and 2015, as you can see in this graph:

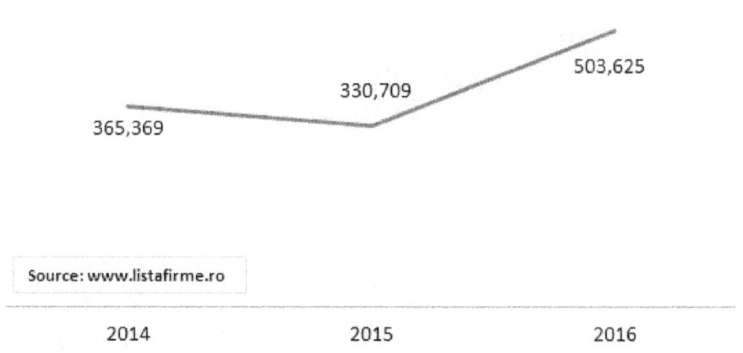

Year 2016 confirmed the new business model via company revenues. According to

---

[67] This value includes: design and topography costs, authorization costs, cost of the building, cost of the heating system, cost of equipment and the cost of goods to be sold. As of 27 May 2017, 1 euro equals 4.55 ron.

internal information, Sticky Store acquired the following turnover: in 2014 sales of 34,270 RON; in 2015 sales of 107,029 RON and in 2016 sales of 204,923 RON. However, so as to foster Sticky store growth and Sarcom Distribution implicitly, specific actions should be taken with regard to marketing functional strategy. Thus, besides traditional advertisement campaigns by using flyers-which were tremendously beneficial for Stick store- and world-of-mouth, using online marketing instruments and tactics represents an opportunity which cannot be missed.

Company objective with regard to online marketing activities is to inform as many potential customers as it's possible about Sticky Store which is located in Râmnicu Vâlcea city and to provide information about Sticky and Coral products. This objective has been agreed on taking into consideration customer's behavior changes with regard to new methods and capabilities of acquiring information via Internet. One important thing is that Sticky brand is very well-known locally, which is an aspect we have to capitalize on.

III.2. Marketing environment analysis

Clearly identifying marketing environment is vital for every organization either we talk about a private company or a public institution. An organization can't act randomly, in a continuous fog, without having a direction for development and a plan to follow. Whether the organization is aware or not, it acts based on a pattern which sometimes is instinctual and sometimes is short-term oriented.

When we look at small and medium organizations, the manager is the one who analyzes marketing environment and implements actions which may ensure a higher or lower competitiveness. However, in these small organizations, there is barely a strategy which may state certain steps to be followed in order to ensure organization development; we usually find a mix of ideas, actions and plans which can be combined in a functional strategy. This is also the case of Sarcom Distribution Ltd. where a functional online marketing strategy exists and it is composed of a mix between different instruments and tactics peculiar to online marketing.

A marketing specialist should have an in-depth vision of the organization and its marketing environment and I think the following ought to be taken into consideration: internal analysis, external analysis, S.W.O.T. analysis and price analysis. Thus, in my study, I have applied these analyses to Sarcom Distribution Ltd.

With regard to **internal analysis**, I consider the following as being the most important elements: human resources, material resources, management capabilities, internal organization, product policy, price policy, promotion policy, placement policy, vision, mission and long-term objectives.

Human resources are the most important asset of every organization. Nowadays Romanian business environment has not fully understood human resources value and potential, especially when we talk about reaching medium and long term objectives. An efficient human resources management can ensure organization progress and knowledge sharing or, conversely, can lead to failure. With regard to Sarcom Distribution Ltd., there are just two employees. Therefore, based on employees' skills, studies and professional background, at the company level there is knowledge of economics, English language skills, digital competencies and social and human sciences. Taking into consideration company activity profile, based on employees' capabilities, the company may try enlarging its activities or diversifying.

Company's material resources are the following: a car(~4000 euro), a van(~3500 euro), a store(~20.000 euro) and specific equipment(~2500 euro). An important intangible resource-which is not owned by the company but helps it a lot- is represented by Sticky and Coral brands.

With regard to management and internal organization, all decisions are taken by common consent after analyzing the situation and identifying the best solution for the company. An important result of management and decision implementation process is the online marketing functional strategy. Within the company, knowledge sharing concept has been implemented and this has led to a high degree of flexibility.

Let's have a look at Sarcom Distribution Ltd. marketing mix:
- Product policy: Our portofolio includes alchidic paints, primers, alchidic varnishes, water-based varnishes, diluents, washable paints, adhesives, decorative paints, dyes and pigments, road marking paints and auxiliary products.
- Price policy: Taking into consideration that this company is the official distributor of Sarcom Ltd-which is the producer- we can offer the best price for our customers.
- Promotion policy: Promotion policy is composed of online and offline activities. Among other offline activities, the distribution of flyers has shown us that it is the best way to promote the Sticky Store and its products within Râmnicu Vâlcea city. With regard to

online environment, I have implemented a large number of instruments and tactics so as to enhance company awareness locally. This year, one big flyer campaign will be realized again, combined with the most efficient online marketing instruments and tactics.
- Placement policy: We sell Sticky and Coral products using two different ways: via Sticky Store and via distribution channel-retailers-.

Company **vision** can be synthetized and the following ideas result: We think people appreciate the experience they have when buying something, so we capitalize on this. If we manage to create a special relation between us and our customers, they will prefer doing business with us, even if we are a small company as compared to local competitor like Dedeman or Leroy Merlin-which is supposed to open a store this year-.

Company mission is providing to potential customers the best prices and specialty pieces of advice with regard to its products. The company has already fulfilled its mission and it has to maintain it over time.

On medium or long term- 3 or 4 years- the company aims to achieve continuous growth of revenues, together with an increase in Sticky store awareness. I think this objective is likely to be achieved at least for 2017, taking into consideration the economic context.

We consider that our competitive advantage is composed of four elements: best prices, free delivery for large orders, specialty pieces of advice and strong customer oriented approach to doing business.

When it comes to **external analysis**, we ought to focus on two main directions: micro-environment and macro-environment.

Thus, micro-environment elements like suppliers, middlemen, customers and competitors are relevant for the company.

The macro-environment elements which I consider to be relevant for the company are the following: demographic environment, economic environment, technologic environment, politic environment, cultural environment and natural environment.

I consider is better to have a look at the elements which constitute Sarcom Distribution Ltd. marketing **micro-environment** so as to see what is specific to this company:

- **Suppliers:** Sarcom Distribution Ltd. has two main suppliers, namely Sarcom Ltd for all Sticky and Coral products and Catanoiu Ltd for auxiliary products and tools. In this category I have also included accounting services supplier and electricity supplier.

- **Middlemen:** Sarcom Distribution Ltd does not have middlemen; all products are sold directly based on business relation like Business to Customer, Business to Government or Business to Business. Promotion activities are performed by company employees based on their knowledge; therefore the company does not have any promotion middleman. However, the company has financial intermediaries: Transilvania Bank and treasury.
- **Customers:** Nowadays, the company has three business relations: Business-2-Business with producers which use its products during production processes and retailers; Business-2-Customer which is established within Sticky store via retail; Business-2-Government with public institutions via electronic public procurement service.
- **Competitors:** With regard to competitors, the direct competition is represented by brands like: Oskar, Kober, Spor and Casa Bella. For Sarcom Distribution Ltd., from Sticky store perspective, the biggest local competitor is Dedeman store. I have made two price analyses in order to better observe the situation: the first analysis compares similar products-Sticky products versus

competitors' products- and the second compares Sticky products' prices within Stick store versus Dedeman store.

The next table shows Sticky products prices as compared to competitors' similar products prices; information source is Dedeman[68] website. These are the only products which can be directly compared, because the others have different features according to raw materials quality, quantity and technical features.

Product	Sticky Price (in Dedeman store)	Oskar Price	Kober Price
Vopsea lavabila exterior 15L	123.80 RON	329.00 RON	138.00 RON
Vopsea lavabila interior 15L	72.90 RON (17L)	189.00 RON	69.64 RON
Vopsea lavabila interior 8.5L	48.60 RON	125.00 RON	40.38 RON
Lac pentru lemn 0.75 L	15.28 RON	20.08 RON	19.02 RON
Amorsa 4L	18.41 RON	38.38 RON	35.62 RON

Table 1: Similar products price analysis

---

[68] www.dedeman.ro, accessed on 21 May 2017.

Because Dedeman store is the main competitor of Sticky store, analyzing Sticky products' prices is fairly relevant.

Unlike Dedeman store, Sticky store has the whole product portofolio available to be sold, which is just one advantage. The information has been obtained using Dedeman website and Sarcom Distribution Ltd. internal documents:

Product	Sticky store Price	Dedeman store Price
Sticky Bronzalchid 0.75L	13.50 RON	16.18 RON
Prenadez Sticky 0.5L	9 RON	10.29 RON
Amorsa 1L	3 RON	3.72 RON
Amorsa 4L	11 RON	12.89 RON
Amorsa 10L	23.50 RON	23.79 RON
Vopsea lavabila exterior 15L	109 RON	123.80 RON
Vopsea lavabila interior 15L	74 RON	72.90 RON
Pigment culoare	9 RON	9.91 RON
Grund alchidic pentru protectia lemnului	10 RON	10.38 RON

Diluant unviersal 509 0.5L	5 RON	5.11 RON
Lac alchidic 0.75L	15.50 RON	15.28 RON
Vopsea alchidica 0.6L diferite nuante	8 RON	7.90 RON
Vopsea lavabila antimucegai 8.5L	63.50 RON	67.07 RON

Table 2: Stick store versus Dedeman store prices

I consider is better to have a look at the elements which constitute Sarcom Distribution Ltd. marketing **macro-environment** so as to see what is specific to this company:

• **Demographic environment:** According to latest information, Romania has a population of 19.82 million people with a downward trend (-0.4%)[69]. Vâlcea county had in 2011 a population of 371,714 people, of whom 180,912 men and 190.802 women[70]; Râmnicu Vâlcea city has a population of around 90,000 people. Population

---

[69] România Liberă, *INS: Populația României, în continuă scădere și tot mai îmbătrânită*, available at http://romanialibera.ro/actualitate/eveniment/populatia-romaniei-este-in-continua-scadere-si-tot-mai-imbatranita-426622?c=q2561, accessed on 21 May 2017.

[70] B.N.R., *Monografia judetului Valcea*, available at https://www.google.ro/url?sa=t&rct=j&q=&esrc=s&source=web&cd=9&cad=rja&uact=8&ved=0ahUKEwji2Kjuu_7TAhWHvRQKHUq5BUgQFghpMAg&url=http%3A%2F%2Fbnr.ro%2FDocumentInformation.aspx%3FidInfoClass%3D13567%26idDocument%3D19932%26directLink%3D1&usg=AFQjCNGL9ruFlvcKlYv8iufM_SzemOzF2g&sig2=x9osSmtmu75SrnJqeyK7bw, accessed on 21 May 2017, pag. 6.

structure shows a phenomenon of population aging: in 2014 14.9% of population had an age between 0 and 14, 70% of population had an age between 15 and 64, and 15.1% of population had an age of 65 or above[71]. According to the National Institute of Statistics, life expectancy is around 75 years with an upward trend after 1989. Based on general trend, economic conditions and limited development possibilities of Vâlcea county, I think its population will decrease with approximately 0.5% yearly.

• **Economic environment:** It deeply influences organizations and people behavior. There are a lot of factors which need to be analyzed so as to obtain a correct image about which conditions an organization acts in, such as: the perspective of getting a properly paid and stable job, currency stability, prices level, inflation rate, purchasing power, interest rate and so forth. Romanian economic general state is good and World Bank[72] economic forecasts on short term are positive: fiscal easing measures, V.A.T. of

---

[71] I.N.S., *Anuarul demografic al României*, available at http://www.insse.ro/cms/files/publicatii/pliante%20statistice/Anuarul_demografic-PROMO.pdf, accessed on 21 May 2017.
[72] World Bank, *Romania Overview*, available at http://www.worldbank.org/en/country/romania/overview#3, accessed on 22 May 2017.

19% and the increase with 16% of minimum wage are the principal conditions which impel nowadays economic environment. Another important indicator for the company is the average net salary which had a value of 2,300 Rons[73] in February 2017.

- **Technological environment:** Technological environment influences all life aspects. Either we talk from producer or consumer perspective, new technologies can create development opportunities. The main advantage for the company is represented by the high Internet penetration level which has led to changes in customer behavior. Thus, the customer uses new communication technologies-e.g. laptops, smartphones, tablets- to search for information, spends more time on Internet and social networks and even buys from online platforms. For Sarcom Distribution, the most important aspects of technological environment and its progresses is represented by online marketing capabilities. Fast technological progresses force us as marketing specialists to be always informed on business environment and keep an eye on

---

[73] Libertarea.ro, *INS: Salariul mediu net in ianuarie 2017 a fost de 2.300 lei*, available at http://www.libertatea.ro/stiri/salariul-mediu-net-in-ianuarie-2017-1771757, accessed on 22 May 2017.

the instruments and tactics which may be used to enhance businesses: Search Engine Marketing, Social Media Marketing, Website Marketing, Search Engine Optimization, Content Marketing and so forth.

- **Political environment:** Romanian political environment is favorable for economic development, even if there are still some problems with regard to corruption and organized crime. As a nation, we should capitalize on our strategic position in Eastern European and focus on durable development and compliance with common European values. Through this way we can stimulate economic initiative and foreign direct investments. The regulations, governmental agencies' activity and lobby groups are also entities which can change business environment to a lesser or greater extent. From the perspective of an economic agent, a good understanding of political trends and implicitly what the political parties want to implement when it comes to public policies, ensures a better decisional knowledge base.
- **Cultural environment:** The cultural environment represents all material and spiritual values which were created by mankind and the institutions

which are required to promote these values. If we looked at national level, we would observe that each state has its own particularities. The cultural environment influences business environment and especially the marketing activities: for example, the same advertisement would be perceived differently by a Romanian as compared to a Nigerian and an English joke may not be understood by a Romanian. What is important for my study is that one should always know the cultural environment within which he will do business. For Sarcom Distribution Ltd. this aspect is clear, being a Romanian company which deal only with Romanian customers.

•**Natural environment:** The main short and medium term problem remains the pollution. More or less known, the pollution affects the Earth and each negative action is costly to be compensated. As compared to other states, Romania is doing well with regard to this problem. All organization should take care when it comes to pollution reduction and respect the regulations. Problems like energetic resources and petroleum price will still be present on medium term. For sure, there are also problems like: deforestation, global water consumption and its availability, equity of resource allocation, acid rain and last but not least, food availability and its distribution.

Here is the S.W.O.T. analysis of Sarcom Distribution Ltd., which I have made for the company:

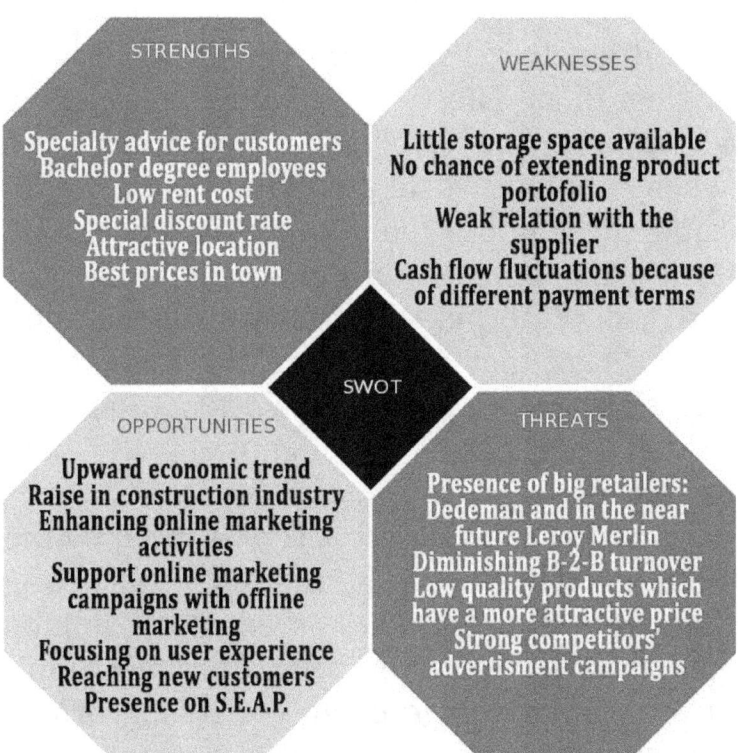

Figure 3: S.W.O.T. analysis of Sarcom Distribution Ltd.

Therefore, by analyzing different factors which influence to a lesser or greater extent the company, I consider that on short and medium term there is a favorable economic environment for the company to grow; it is also very important that online and offline marketing activities should be a continuous point of focus for ensuring company growth.

III.3. Using online marketing instruments and tactics for promoting Sarcom Distribution Ltd.

Either we like it or not, the world is changing in an alert pace. Lately, the online environment has evolved dramatically and nowadays half of world population is online. In Europe, three out of four people have access to Internet and spend more than 30 hours per month on Internet. The same information source[74] says that almost one third of online spent time is on social networks; thus, this potential shouldn't be ignored by any organization.

Another vital aspect is represented by the interconnectivity of online marketing instruments and tactics. For example, linking organization's website with organization's Facebook official page creates a strong bridge between them. Thus, a potential customer can see an advertisement on Facebook and then access organization's website so as to learn more about it or certain products. Therefore, each change to website marketing, social media

---

[74] Atelierul Digital, *Lumea trece la mediul digital*, available at https://learndigital.withgoogle.com/atelieruldigital/lesson/24, accessed on 18 April 2017.

marketing or search engine marketing has an impact on other elements.

Every organization can use online marketing instruments and tactics according to its objectives. The objectives should be clearly defined and allow crafting an action plan: marketing specialists usually choose a mix of instruments and tactics to achieve their goals. It is important we should realize that every marketing action ought to be viewed from two perspectives: organization's perspective and potential customer's perspective.

With regard to Sarcom Distribution Ltd., the main objective is to create online presence and promote its store named Sticky store. In order to achieve this purpose, online marketing instruments and tactics-website marketing, social media marketing and search engine marketing- will be integrated, synchronized and adjusted permanently. **Website marketing** specific actions are the first step in crafting online presence.

The first thing which needs to be done is to create a pin on Google Maps on the exact business location. Through this way, when a potential customer searches for the organization, its headquarters will appear in search results. I also recommend providing information with regard to: work schedule, complete address, prices, services and some photos.

Google search engine doesn't require the organization to have a website or a social network page for showing it among search results. For crafting a powerful online presence both website and social network page- Facebook- are required because their existence influences Google search results: an organization which owns a website and a Facebook page besides other online marketing instruments and tactics enjoys better online visibility and higher positions in search engine's results.

Taking into consideration all the possibilities of creating a website, I concluded that the best option is to call on a website platform builder company which offers an easy interface for creating and adjusting your website. After analyzing the alternatives I found out that the best choice for Sarcom Distribution Ltd. was weebly.com platform. The cost of domain and hosting services is around 200 Rons per year and it is really a bargain. Here are some advantages of using weebly.com platform:

- It provides an intuitive interface;
- Various large templates collection;
- Free website mobile version;
- Content management system;
- SEO capabilities;
- Large website customization possibilities. You can add to your website elements like: title bar, text,

images, gallery, presentations, maps, contact forms, survey forms, buttons, news feed, embedded code, documents, youtube clips, audio files, video files, social icons, RSVP forms, feed reader and search box.
- E-commerce capabilities
- Google AdSense.

After I analyzed product portofolio, free web domains and thinking what a potential customer would search for, I have taken the decision of buying www.vopselevalcea.com domain. When designing the website, I aimed to provide relevant information for customers and ensuring a great user experience. Elements such as landing page, menu, website structure, photos, interactive elements, contact details, content, in-site links and high quality information are key points on which I have put emphasis. Taking into consideration that the potential customer enters our website in order to gather information about Sticky store or a certain product, I tried to develop an intuitive website structure, combined with a consequent design.

Therefore, I have developed and implemented the following website structure:

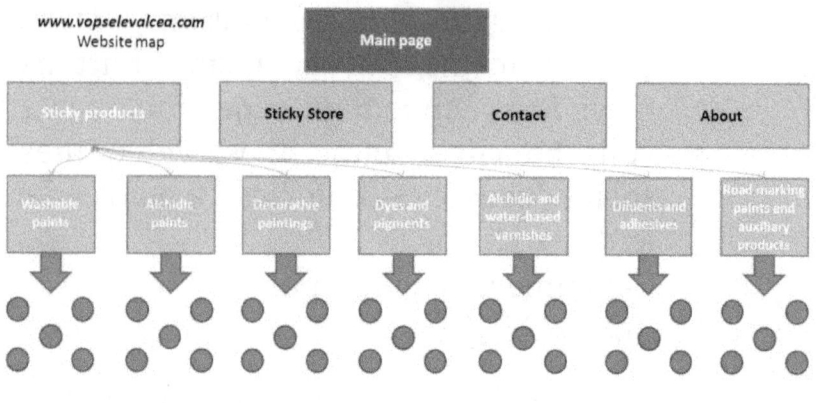

Figure 4: www.vopselevalcea.com Website map

The website has been operational since 2015, but the period which is analyzed for enhancing this particular website through different online marketing instruments and tactics is from July 2016 to May 2017. Every month of the previously mentioned interval metrics have been taken and I focused on three main indicators: average page views per day, average unique visitors per day and website traffic source.

Considering the way search engines index each website, I decided that every page should offer both technical information and product instructions, the content becoming in this way valueable for both potential customers and search engines. Each product description has strategically place phases so as to enhance the website visibility on search engine results.

During optimization process, according to best practices in website marketing, I have put interactive go-back buttons on every page, I have realized hyperlink[75] connections with auxiliary products and I have implemented alt-text[76] function for all product images. I have also respected the content marketing concept, which mainly refers to information quality and uniqueness as seen through potential customer's eyes.

In the optimization process, an important place was occupied by search engines. I have acted with regard to two main directions: search engine optimization and search engine marketing. Search Engine Optimization refers to the adjustment of certain website code lines in a way that boosts website visibility so as to get a better position in search organic results when someone searches for the organization or its products/services. Therefore, an efficient search engine optimization implementation should assure that the search engine finds the website, understands it and offers it a place in search results hierarchy: the higher is website's position in organic search results, the better has search engine optimization been done. The biggest advantage of search engine optimization is that the whole process is free, and

---

[75] Hyperlink connections allow users to navigate to a certain page within website by clicking on a certain text, usually a blue one.
[76] Alt-text functions help search engine to understand and index an image. Basically, you teach the search engine what the image is about.

weebly.com platform offers the possibility of implementing it. Search engine marketing-related actions will be presented later in this study.

In order to apply the most suitable search engine optimization tactics, a marketing specialist should firstly understand how a search engine works. When a user makes a search, the search engine identifies within its data base-which is composed of indexed websites- which words match the ones previously typed by the user, ranks the websites and delivers them to the user. No matter what search engine we are talking about, it fulfills the following three functions[77]: examines website content, classifies website content and classifies websites accordingly. Thus, I have implemented in each page's title and content certain keywords which are characteristic to company's products. Keywords are chosen according to their search frequency, competition, relevance and also based on the rule of thumb. A useful instrument which I have used is Google Search Console. It offers information about: search statistics, which keywords are used, how many users have seen the website within search results, how many users have clicked on the website link and so forth.

---

[77] These functions are also the main reason why search engine optimization is so important.

Summarizing, I have taken the following actions in the search engine optimization process: I have defined keywords for the website and its constitutive subpages, I have inserted in every product description certain words-which I have placed in strategically chosen places-, I have implemented Google Search Console[78] and I have built and submitted the website map to Google so as to enhance indexing process.

In the period July 2016-February 2017, the average pageviews/day was as the following graph shows:

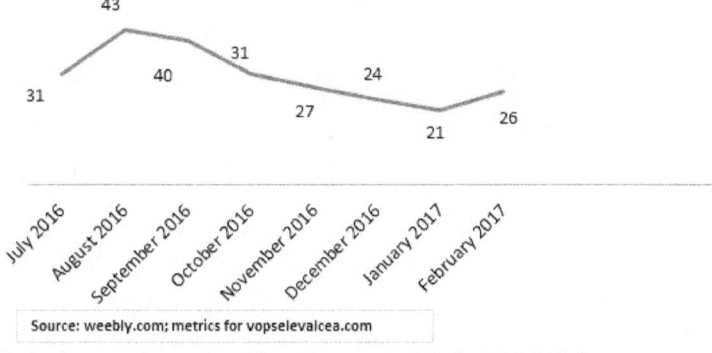

Figure 5: Average pagevies/day for period July2016-February 2017

In the same period, the average unique visitors/day was:

---

[78] This search engine optimization instrument provides information with regard to the number of visitors who reached the website as a consequence of making a search via search engine. It also provides information about which keywords lead to the website, average click rate, average search position and so forth.

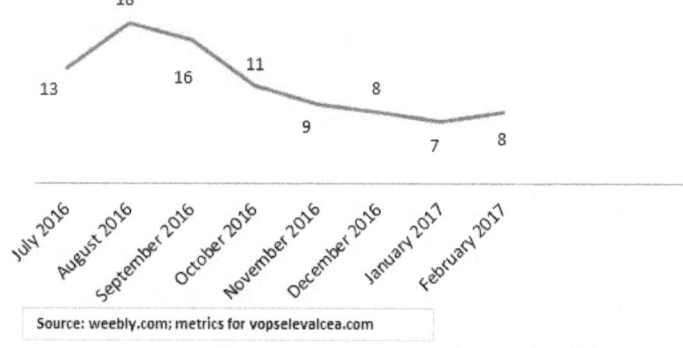

Figure 6: Average unique visitors/day for period July 2016- February 2017

Another important aspect is given by website traffic source. According to internal company reports provided by Google Analytics[79], the first three traffic sources are the following: direct traffic, organic search traffic and social media traffic.

The optimization process required some technical adjustments as I previously mentioned and it was ended at the end of February; its results may be observed during the following months, **March**, **April** and **May**. The results recorded during these months are also influenced by the actions which I have taken with regard to search engine marketing and social media marketing. At the end of this chapter I presented information about page

---

[79] Google Analytics is a freemium web analytics service offered by Google that tracks and reports website traffic. It's quite easy to be implemented and is a powerful online marketing tool.

views per day and unique visitors per day evolution.

The actions which I have taken with regard to **search engine marketing** were aimed to rise website visibility, to rise website traffic and consequently to improve Stick store and Sticky products awareness. As it is the most used search engine, I have used Google search engine to achieve my goals and Google Adwords[80] was the tool.

Either we talk about search engine marketing or social media marketing, a very important concept is the geo-localized promotion. We can easily agree that technology, and especially online advertisement, has changed the interaction pattern between sellers and buyers, marketing specialists having nowadays more and more powerful and versatile instruments. Geo-localized promotion offers the possibility of better targeting areas where one wants his advert to be shown. Thus, I considered that a radius of 20 kilometers having the center within Râmnicu Vâlcea town would be enough for Google Adwords campaign.

Through search engine marketing activities, adverts are run among first places of a search result whenever a user looks for

---

[80] Google AdWords is Google's advertising system in which advertisers bid on certain keywords in order for their clickable ads to appear in Google's search results.

something via the search engine, using a specific keyword. Thus, the company can bid for that keyword and the advert will be shown. The best thing when running a Google Adwords campaign is that the organization is billed only if the user clicks on the ad-Pay Per Click advertising-. Unlike traditional promotions, search engine marketing provides great targeting capabilities and enables you to reach people who are interested in your products.

There are some things you need to know so as to successfully implement a search engine campaign through Google Adwords: advert position is given by bid value-it is established by the marketing specialist- and relevance-it is established through keyword-; defining and choosing the right keywords is utterly important-you can obtain great information whereby Google Search Console and/or you can also define your own keywords based on rule of thumb-; search engine marketing should be implemented only after website marketing processes, optimizations and tactics are done.

I have identified the following advantages of using Google Adwords:
- Raises website visitors;
- Allows ad delivery only to interested people by using specific keywords;
- Allows geo-location settings;
- Offers four options of promotion: search ads, display ads, video ads and app ads;

- Pay Per Click system.

On 29 April 2017 I started a Google Adwords campaign for a period of two weeks, until 13 May 2017. I set the following features for the campaign so as to reach my goal-enhancing Sticky store and its products awareness locally-:
- 20 kilometers radius having the center of Râmnicu Vâlcea town;
- Cost of 10 RON per day having a bid strategy of maximizing clicks on ad;
- Advert placement in search network and display network for all devices;
- The keywords which triggered the ad- are written in Romanian language, obviously-: tencuiala decorativa, vopsea lavabila, lavabila exterior, lavabila interior, tencuiala decorativa sticky, vopsea decorativa, vopsea lavabila exterior, vopsea lavabila interior, vopsea exterior, vopsea lavabila sticky, vopsea sticky, magazinul sticky, sarcom valcea, lac sticky, vopsele valcea, lavabila interior sticky, lavabila exterior sticky, sticky valcea, lac exterior, lac pentru lemn, lac pe baza de apa, lavabila sticky.

Here is how the advert looked like when it was served as a response to a search enquiry based on above-mentioned keywords:

Figure 7: Google Adwords advert example

When analyzing the results for Sarcom Distribution Adwords campaign, two indicators are relevant. The first is called "impressions" and counts how many times the advert was shown without being clicked on; I once again say that Google Adwords works based on Pay Per Click system, which means one pays only when a user clicks the ad regardless of impressions value. Thus, a high impression value is favorable because even if the user didn't click on advert, it would remain in his mind and during the next time period the chance of recognizing the company or the product which were to be advertised rises. The second indicator is called "clicks" and as you have probably guessed it shows how many times the advert was clicked on; it also represents the base of calculus for billing.

Google Adwords campaign results were the following: 1.301 impressions, 105 clicks with an average cost per click of 1.34 RON and average position 1.4. The upshot of this campaign is that through this way, I managed to increase the traffic on the company website and thus enhanced its online presence. Google Adwords campaigns are best for e-commerce websites, which is not Sarcom Distribution's case, its website being an informative one. However, the impressions were quite numerous and I'm sure that "Magazinul Sticky" will remain in the memory of at least some of those who have seen the ad. The following graph shows the evolution of clicks and impressions each day:

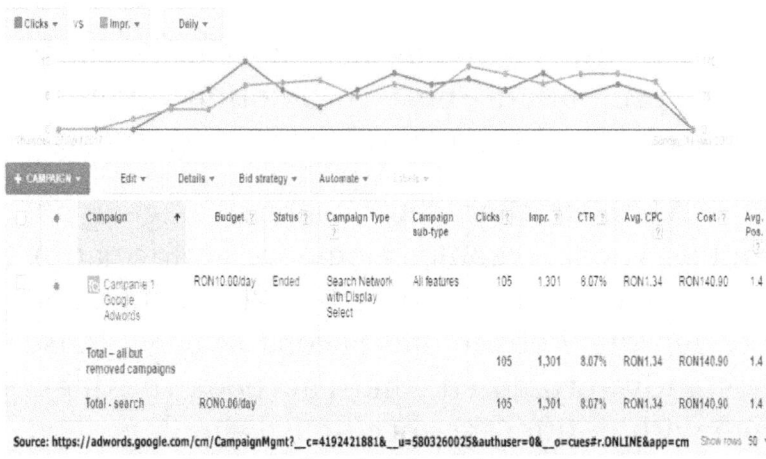

Figure 8: Google Adwords metrics

With regard to **social media marketing**, I have the same objectives: enhancing company's online presence, namely promoting Sticky store and Sticky products. I created a Facebook page for this company in 2015 because I had realized the importance of social media and the opportunity of using it for engaging with potential customers. When I created the social media page, I took into account the advantages of being present within social media, especially Facebook:

- Presence on the most well-known social media platform;
- Strategic advantages over competitors ;
- Low promotion costs ;
- Information gathering capabilities;
- Better targeting;
- News delivery capabilities for interested audience;
- Multiple promotion possibilities: page promotion, post promotion, website promotion and viral marketing.

When crafting the Facebook page I put emphasis on graphic elements, information quality and tried to strengthen the connection between the website and Facebook page. I also constantly promoted the Facebook business page within different specific Facebook groups. Through this way on 2 May 2017, the company had a feedback of 4.9 out of 5, 21 people were there, 1080 followers and 1083 likes[81]. Please keep in mind that whoever likes a Facebook page, also subscribes to that page newsletter, which is an important aspect for a business as it may enlarge its audience.

In other words, I implemented the following social media marketing instruments: viral marketing, page promotion, post promotion and website promotion.

---

[81] Information source: https://www.facebook.com/vopselevalcea/

Viral marketing is a method of marketing whereby consumers are encouraged to share information about a company's goods or services via Internet. Facebook provides the best framework for implementing viral marketing campaigns. The first step for implementing a viral marketing campaign was the initiation of a contest from 17 March 2017 to 7 April 2017, having as prize free products up to a value of approximately 75 Rons. The contest was aimed only at Vâlcea county residents and its rules of participation were designed by me in such a way so as to maximize contest promotion and sharing. The same type of contest was previously implemented in 2015 and 2016, exclusively on Facebook, having the purpose of consolidating company presence on this social network.

The second step for implementing the viral marketing campaign was contest post promotion which contained contest photo and participation instructions. Based on my experience, I recommend that the contest image should be relevant for the organization and participation instructions easy to be followed. In order to maximize campaign impact, I have included the requirement of sharing the contest post within contest rules: this way each participant needed to share to his friends the contest post, thus promoting it and the company. Through this tactic, the contest post reached participants' friends and encouraged them to participate too. With regard to previous contests, in 2015 there were 25 participants and in 2016 there were 40 participants. During 20 March and 3 April 2017 I promoted the contest post, setting the following features: both men and women aged 20-65+ were targeted, Râmnicu Vâlcea city and a 25 kilometers radius, budget of 86 Rons. Thus, the viral marketing campaign cost 161 Rons-prize cost + contest post promotion cost-.

The viral marketing campaign results were astonishing:

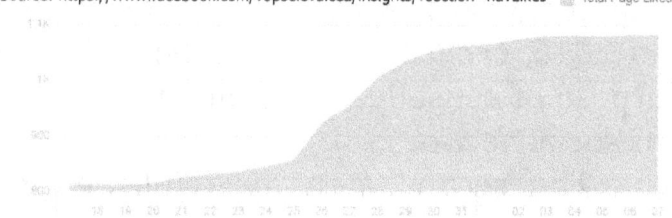

Figure 9: Facebook page likes evolution 18th of March 2017 to 7th of April 2017

The number of Sarcom Distribution Ltd Facebook page likes soared from 812 on 17 March 2017 to 1082 on 7 April 2017, overall Facebook page audience being thus enlarged. As you can observe from Figure 10, the post had an audience of 20,153 people, out of whom 8,339 people were paid audience and the rest of 11,814 people organic audience. By using viral marketing, the contest post had an effect of snowball, its good performance being reflected even in website statistics.

Via viral marketing I have managed to obtain 222 contest participants[82], 448 contest likes, 269 contest comments, 291 contest shares and 270 new company's Facebook page likes. To conclude, viral marketing is a very efficient online marketing instrument which is characterized by reduced costs and a stark impact:

Figure 10: Viral marketing metrics

Because of its high efficiency, I have taken the decision to implement another viral marketing campaign for Sarcom Distribution Ltd. this year, with a double budget and at a proper time.

---

[82] Vopsele Valcea – Magazinul Sticky Facebook Page, available at https://www.facebook.com/vopselevalcea/photos/a.721591127876222.1073741831.705487959486539/1318891498146179/?type=3&theater, accessed on 3 May 2017.

With regard to **page promotion** activity, on 2 May 2017 I set up a campaign of Vopsele Valcea – Magazinul Sticky page promotion within Facebook social media. I targeted people aged between 18 and 65+, both genders, within Râmnicu Vâlcea city and +10 miles radius. The promotion started on 2 May 2017 and ended on 9 May 2017. With regard to the budget, I considered 14 Rons per day would do the trick and Facebook estimated that for this amount I would get at least 13 new likes per day, which means obtaining around 91 new likes at the end of this campaign.

Page promotion campaign results can be observed in this graph:

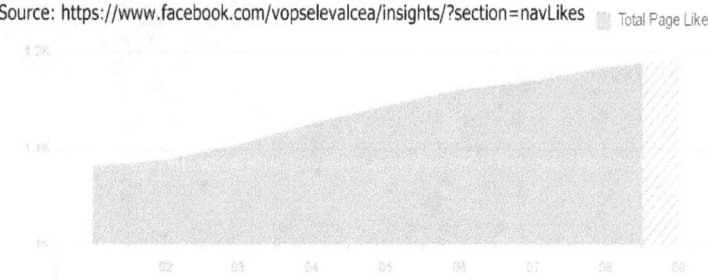

Figure 11: Page promotion campaign metrics

During 2 May 2017 and 9 May 2017 total page likes rose from 1,082 to 1,193. Therefore, page promotion campaign efficiency was better than Facebook had estimated: 111 new likes instead of 91, which means 111 new people who subscribed to Sarcom Distribution Ltd Facebook page and appreciated Sticky store.

According to the information Facebook provided for the company, page promotion campaign has reached 4,580 people. Even if they hadn't liked the Vopsele Valcea – Magazinul Sticky Facebook page, they would remember at least something about Sticky store or at least know about its existence. The image which I used for running this page promotion campaign was a simple one because Facebook doesn't allow images with a lot of embedded text to be used for promotions; this way it tries to boost campaign efficiency. I have put at the end of my study the image which I have used for page promotion campaign to serve as an indicative example[83]. During page promotion I have also observed an increase in unique website visitors number and page views number, this way being once again confirmed the interconnectivity of online marketing instruments.

With regard to **post promotion** social media marketing instrument, on 10th of May 2017, I set up a post promotion campaign on Facebook. I strongly recommend that the post should have a relevant image[84] containing company contact data and expressing the main business idea. Besides the image, the post should have some text which has to be concise and tempt a potential customer to discover the

---

[83] See annex number 6.
[84] See annex number 7.

organization; therefore I have chosen the following text: "Va asteptam la magazinul Sticky pentru a descoperi produsele noastre! www.vopselevalcea.com #vopselevalcea #magazinulsticky". It's a good idea to include organization website in post description because the user will be thus encouraged to click on it and learn more about your organization and products. Hash tags are also useful for establishing common elements between different Facebook posts.

Post promotion may be made by two ways: either by sharing the post within certain Facebook groups-I have shared this post in 7 local Facebook groups, which is quite a large number taking into account that Râmnicu Vâlcea is a fairly small city- which are proper for its audience or you may pay Facebook to run a post promotion campaign. So as to maximize campaign efficiency I've implemented both measures and I recommend you should do the same.

With regard to post promotion using Facebook boost post option, I have targeted people aged between 18 and 65+, both genders, within Râmnicu Vâlcea city and a radius of 17 kilometers. The promotion started on 10 May 2017 and ended on 17 May 2017. With regard to the budget, I considered 14 RON/day would do the trick and Facebook estimated that for this amount, the post would reach around 6,000 people within this area. Generally speaking, people who liked the promoted post can be invited by the marketing specialist to appreciate organization Facebook page; thus, this may be another way of building up audience and attracting new customers.

Post promotion results were, let's say, normal. The post has reached 8,122 people (2,173 organic and 5,949 paid), got 234 likes and a total engagement[85] of 503. I have also managed to convert some of post likes into page likes: from 1,196 page likes on 10 May 2017 to 1,215 on 17 May 2017. Here you can easily observe post promotion metrics:

Figure 12: Post promotion metrics

With regard to **website promotion**, this instrument which is provided by Facebook

---

[85] Engagement is an indicator which measures the number of interactions-if there are- between a Facebook user and an advertisement. This indicator is the sum of: post clicks, reactions, comments and shares.

would be perfect if you wanted to lead Facebook potential customers to organization website so as to inform them and eventually convert them into customers. It's also true that via this instrument you can raise company awareness. Another important element is that through website promotion, you strengthen the bound between your organization profile on social media and its website: by doing so, you also enhance your position with search engine results.

    With regard to website promotion using Facebook promote website option, I have targeted people aged between 18 and 65+, both genders, within Râmnicu Vâlcea city and a 10 miles radius. This promotion started on 18 May 2017 and ended on 25 May 2017. With regard to the budget, I considered 14 RON/day would do the trick and Facebook estimated that for this amount, the website would get minimum 28 clicks per day, which means a total of around 200 new visitors. This instrument makes is possible to promote organization website on Instagram too.

    Here are the website promotion metrics:

Figure 13: Website promotion metrics

Website promotion campaign results were normal. It reached 6,834 people out of whom 168 accessed the website, 9 appreciated company Facebook page and 5 shared website promotion post. I have also managed to obtain new likes for the company: from 1,215 on 18 May 2017 to 1,224 on 25 May 2017.

Online marketing instruments and tactics which were implemented during March, April and May have significantly enhanced organization image, Stick store image and Sticky products image. The interconnectivity of online marketing instruments and tactics is obvious and the actions that I have taken during my study have enhanced and consolidated Sarcom Distribution Ltd. online presence, as you can infer from these two graphs:

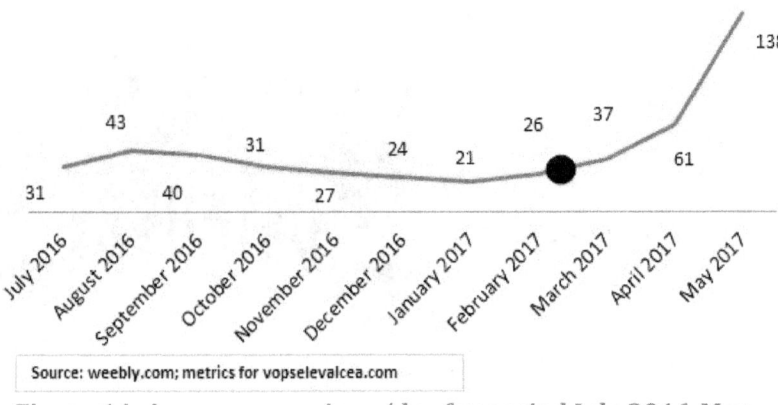

Figure 14: Average pageviews/day for period July 2016-May 2017

Starting with March, you can easily observe online marketing practices impact on website page views per day, which is an important indicator for the organization. As respects unique visitors per day indicator, important improvements were also obtained:

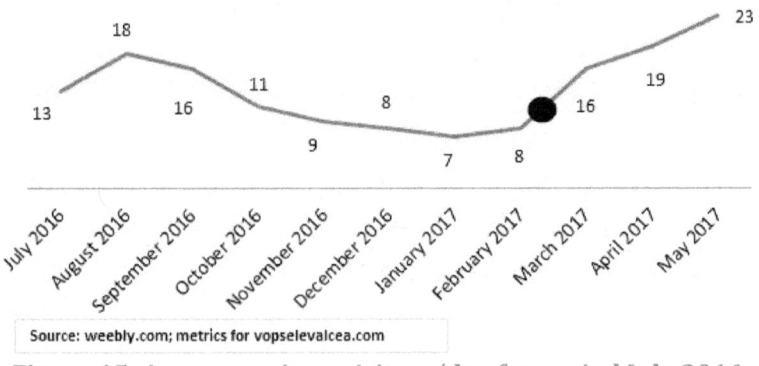

Figure 15: Average unique visitors/day for period July 2016-May 2017

Therefore, online marketing instruments and tactics that I have implemented for Sarcom Distribution Ltd. are a real success. The following objectives have been acquired: enhancing and consolidating company's presence, building online awareness of its Sticky store and last but not least promoting Sticky and Coral products.

Based on my experience in managing online and offline marketing activities, I can strongly assert that each organization has to put online marketing instruments and tactics into a logical form and establish in this way a course of actions, maybe even a short-term oriented online marketing strategy so as to reach its objectives. For Sarcom Distribution Ltd., taking into account its dimensions and available resources, I recommend marketing activities should be focused on both offline methods- promotion using leaflets- and online methods- social media marketing especially-.

Conclusion

As a conclusion, I believe that every organization which wants to take online marketing actions or develop an online marketing plan, should act considering at least three main directions, as I have presented in my study:

1. Website marketing: I consider online presence is sine-qua-non for an organization which aims to develop. By creating a website, every company can provide valuable information like product specifications, instructions, schedule, prices, address, business partners, contact ways, and others for potential customers. It is important to know that just creating a website doesn't assure its success; as I have previously presented, certain optimization activities have to be taken and all online marketing instruments and tactics should be synchronized.
2. Search engine marketing: Generally speaking, I think that using this instrument-I recommend implementing Google Adwords because Google is the most used search engine- enhances

organization visibility in the online environment. In a narrow sense, I have observed that through search engine marketing the organization can obtain advantages as: attracting new customers, better targeting capabilities because of multiple campaign adjustments possibilities, gathering information about what keywords customers use when making an online search, consolidating organization awareness without paying-impressions- and low costs. Even if costs are lower as compared to other marketing practices, please keep in mind that this instrument is quite expensive for a small company and it doesn't worth if the organization doesn't have an e-commerce website.

3. Social media marketing: Social media platforms success represents a huge positive aspect for every marketing specialist. I strongly recommend using Facebook social network because it is the most widely used and short-term perspectives envisage an upward trend in user number evolution. I have showed that any organization can

implement campaigns of viral marketing, post promotion, page promotion and website promotion using Facebook. By doing so, a number of advantages can be obtained, for instance: providing an informational flow for potential customers, gathering customer-related information, enhancing promotion capabilities, raising promotion campaigns efficiency, and even obtaining a competitive advantage over competitors.

References

I. DICTIONARIES AND ENCYCLOPEDIES:

1. Academia Română, *Dicționarul explicativ al limbii române*, Editura Univers Encicplopedic Gold, 2012
2. Dicționarul Economic 2008, Online Edition
3. Dumitrescu, Dan, *Dicționar economic englez-roman*, Editura Akademos Art, 2009
4. Marcu, Florin, *Marele dicționar de neologisme*, Editura Saeculum, 2000
5. New World Encyclopedia, Online Edition

II. SPECIALTY WORKS:

1. Academia Navală "Mircea cel Batran", *Marketing: Note de curs*, Constanta, 2008
2. Atkinson Robert D. And McKay Andrew, *Digital prosperity: Understanding the economic benefits of the information technology revolution*, I.T.I.F., Washington, 2007
3. Bartels, Robert, *The History of Marketing Though*, 2nd Edition, Columbus(Ohio), 1988
4. Băeșu, Camelia, *Economia comerțului – Note de curs-*, Universitatea "Ștefan cel Mare", Suceava, 2012
5. Bășanu Gheorghe, Fundătură Dumitru, *Management și Marketing*, Diacon Coresi Publisher, Bucharest, 1993
6. Boier, Rodica, *Comportamentul consuamtorului*, Graphix publisher, Iași, 1994
7. Chaffey, Dave, *E-business and e-commerce management – Strategy, implementation and practice*, 4th Edition, Prentice Hall, Harlow, 2009
8. Engel J. F. and Blackwell R. D., *Consumer Behavior*, The Dryden Press, Chicago, 1982

9. Gay Richard, Charlesworth Alan and Dr. Esen Rita, *m@rketing on-line: o abordare orientata spre client,* All Publisher, Bucharest, 2009
10. Kotler Philip, Kartajaya Hermanwan, Setiawan Iwan, *marketing 3.0,* John Wiley & Sons, U.S.A., 2010
11. Kotler Philip, Keller Kevin Lane, *Marketing Management,* 14th Edition, Pearson Education, U.S.A., 2012
12. Kotler, Philip, *Managementul marketingului: Analiza, Planificare, Implementare, Control,* Teora Publisher, Bucharest, 1999
13. Mohammed, Rafi, *Internet Marketing,* McGraw Hill, New York, 2004
14. Morariu Daniela, Pizmaş Diana, *Comportamentul consumatorului: dileme, realităţi, perspective,* Editura Bibliofor, Deva, 2001
15. Paţac, Filip, *Istoria comerţului şi turismului,* Editura Eurostampa, Timişoara, 2008
16. Persson, Karl Gunnar, *An economic history of europe,* Cambridge University Press, Cambridge, 2010
17. Rapin, Albert, *Cours de commerce,* Editura Dunod, Paris, 1983
18. Răboacă, Horia Mihai, *Curs de Marketing,* Universitatea Babeş-Bolyai, Cluj-Napoca, 2015
19. Smith, Adam, Inquiry into the nature and causes of the wealth of nations, W. Strahan and T. Cadell, Scotland, 1776
20. Solomon Michael, Bamossy Gary, Askegaard Soren and Hogg Margaret K., *Consumer Behaviour: A european perspective,* Prentice Hall, Harlow, 2006
21. Tecău, Alina Simona, *Comportamentul consumatorului: O privire asupra naturii umane din perspectiva marketingului,* University Press, Bucharest, 2013

22. Temin, Peter, *Inside the business enterprise: historical perspectives on the use of information*, University of Chicago Press, Chicago,1991
23. Teodorescu Nicolae, Iacob Cătoiu, *Comportamentul consumatorului 2nd ed*, Uranus publisher, Bucharest, 2004
24. Timmers, Paul, *Electronic Commerce – Strategies and Models for Business-to-Business Trading*, John Wiley & Sons, 2000
25. Turban E., Lee J., King D. and Chung H.M., *Electronic Commerce: A Managerial Perspective*, Prentice Hall, 1999

III. SPECIALTY STUDIES AND ARTICLES:

1. Belingther Daniel and Cantemir Adrian Călin, *Comportamentul consumatorului digital*, Analele Universității Constantin Brâncuși din Târgu Jiu, Seria Economie, Nr.2/2011
2. European Commission, *Online services, including e-commerce, in the Single Market*, Bruxelles, 2012
3. European Parliament – Directorate general for internal policies, *Study: Consumer behavior in a digital environment*, Bruxelles, 2011
4. Ghent, William James, *The elements of socialism*, The new appeal publisher, Kansas, 1916
5. Jensen, Michael C., *The modern industrial revolution, exit, and the failure of internal control systems*, The journal of finance, Vol. XLVIII, No.3, 1993
6. Katawetawaraks Chayapa and Wang Cheng Lu, *Online Shopper Behavior: Influences of Online Shopping Decision*, Asian Journal of Business Research, Volume 1, Number 2, 2011
7. Laszlo, Kathia Castro, *The evolution of business: learning, innovation and sustainability in the 21st century*, School of Business Administration Press, California, 2001

8. Neti, Sisira, *Social media and its role in marketing,* International Journal of Enterprise Computing and Business Systems, Vol.1 Issue 2, Warangal, July 2011
9. Ovum, *The Future of E-commerce: The Road to 2026,* Online Available Study, New York, 2016
10. Scott, Bruce R., *The political economy of capitalism,* Harvard Business School publications, 2006
11. Sheth Jagdish N., Gardner David M., *History of Marketing Though: An Update,* University of Illinois, 1982
12. Tutorialspoint, E-commerce: electronic commerce approach, Tutorials Point Online Brochure, India, 2014
13. World Trade Organization, *E-commerce in developing countries: opportunities and challenges for small and medium-sized enterprises,* Online Brochure, Switzerland, 2013
14. Zwass, Vladimir, *Electronic Commerce: Structures and Issues,* International Journal of Electronic Commerce, Volume 1, Number 1, Fall, 1996

IV. REGULATIONS AND CODES:

1. Code of Hammurabi, 1750 B.C.
2. Directive 2002/58/CE of European Parliament and Council

V. ONLINE COURSES:

1. Google Academy, Digital Marketing Course
2. Hubspot Academy, Inbound Marketing Course

VI. INTERNET RESOURCES:

1. www.adwords.google.com
2. www.aivr.ro
3. www.ama.org

4. www.dictionar-economic.com
5. www.economist.com
6. www.heidicohen.com
7. www.hubspot.com
8. www.investopedia.com
9. www.kotlermarketing.com
10. www.learndigital.withgoogle.com
11. www.lectiieconomice.net
12. www.libertatea.ro
13. www.link.springer.com
14. www.netmba.com
15. www.sciencedirect.com
16. www.sticky.ro
17. www.technopedia.com
18. www.vopselevalcea.com
19. www.webopedia.com
20. www.weebly.com
21. www.yourarticlelibrary.com
22. www.zf.ro

Annexes

Annex 1:

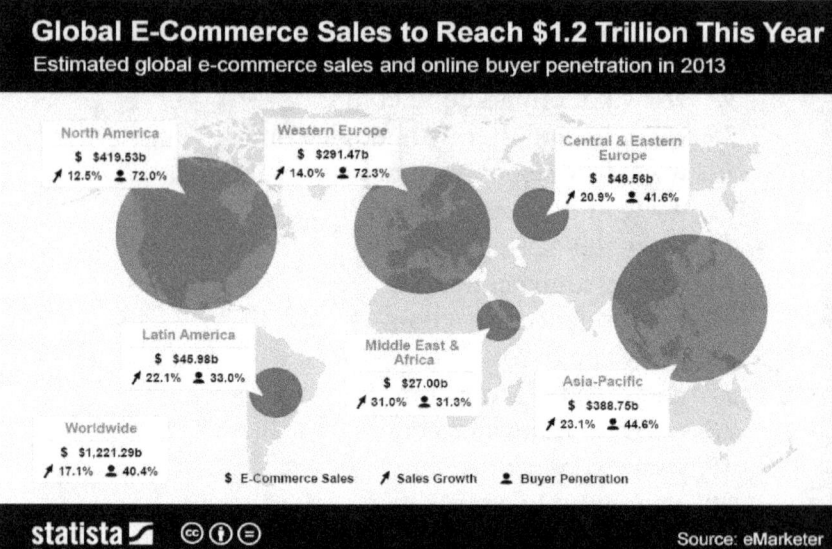

Annex 2:

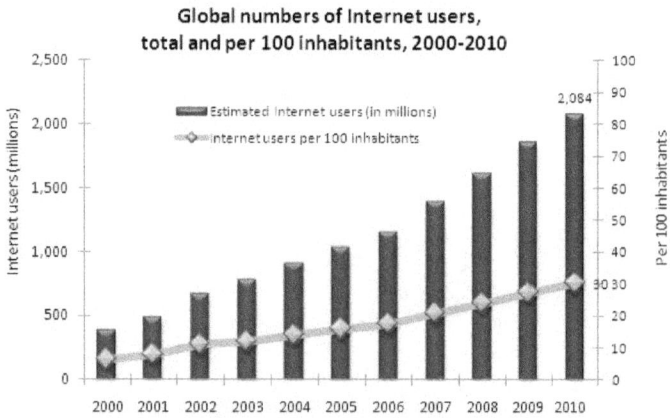

Source: www.itu.int

Annex 3:

Turnover in Romanian e-commerce (in million EUR)

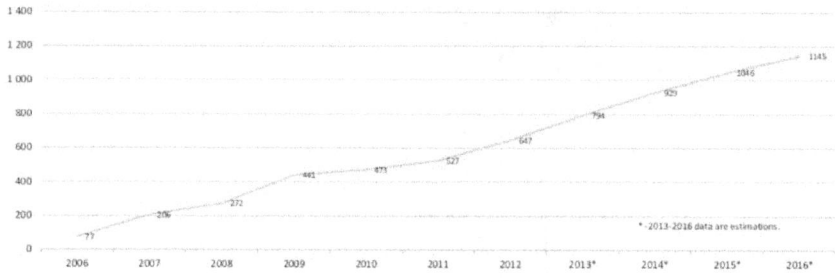

Source: http://www.slideshare.net/gpec/studiu-ecommerce, accessed on 7th of January 2017

Annex 4:

YEAR	Users	Population	% Pop.
2000	800,000	22,217,700	3.6 %
2004	4,000,000	21,377,426	18.7 %
2006	4,940,000	21,154,226	23.4 %
2007	5,062,500	21,154,226	23.9 %
2010	7,786,700	21,959,278	35.5 %
2012	9,642,383	21,848,504	44.1 %

Source: http://www.internetworldstats.com/eu/ro.htm, accessed on 7th of January 2017.

Annex 5:

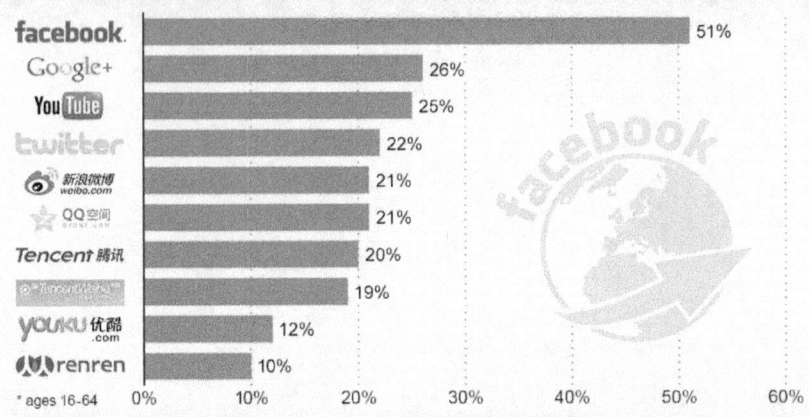

Annex 6:

Annex 7:

Check out these other books written by the same author:

**English for Business Communication
Intercultural Communication
Business Negotiation
Public Relations for Business**

Daniel B. Smith

Click Here to be redirected to Amazon.

[Click Here to be redirected to Amazon](#).

[Click Here to be redirected to Amazon](#).

Click Here to be redirected to Amazon.

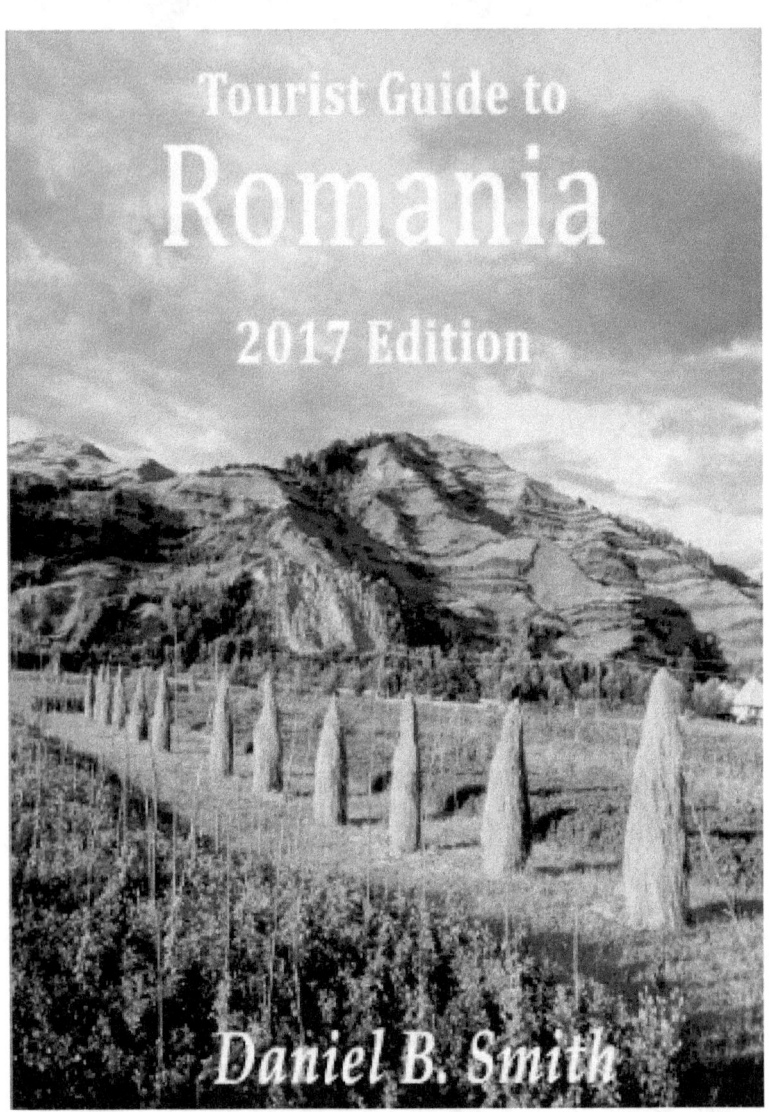

Click Here to be redirected to Amazon.

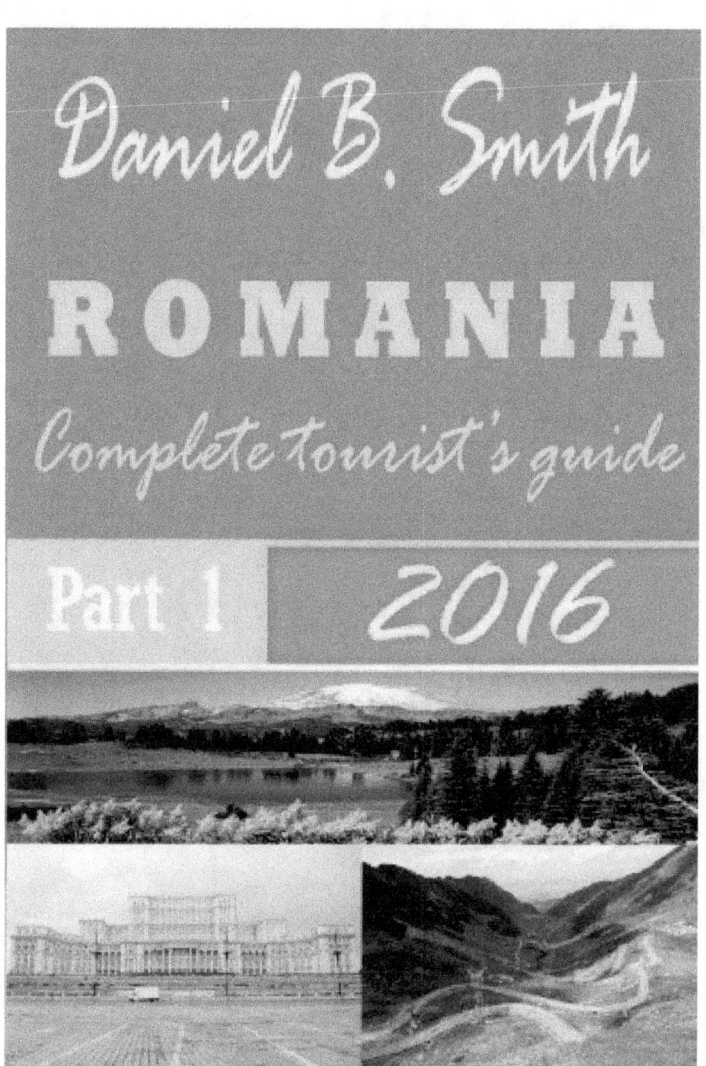

Click Here to be redirected to Amazon.

Click Here to be redirected to Amazon.

Conclusion

In conclusion I want to thank you for buying my book and I hope you will find it useful. Whether you are going to be an assistent manager, manager of a company or an office, reading this book has helped you for sure. One business person nowadays really needs online marketing skills, especially in the globalized market. If one made a step farther and wanted to expand one's business, one would need to be aware of the online marketing instruments and tactics like: social media marketing, website marketing, search engine marketing, e-mail marketing, search engine optimization, content marketing and so forth.

Finally, the case study will show you how to improve your situational awareness, evaluate your possibilities and make the right choice between online marketing tools.

I hope this book worth the money and helped you in becoming better and more knowledgeable.

Write a review

I am constantly improving my books and my work, trying to deliver to my readers the best quality information. To improve my work and myself as a human being, I need organic reviews to know where I am wrong or where I have made mistakes. Remember, there is no such thing as a perfect book, it needs updates all the time, especially if it's digital. If this book has been useful to you, please, write a review with all your thoughts, it won't take more than 1 minute. If you didn't like something from this book, please contact me and I will try to solve your problem.

Honestly,

Daniel B. Smith

www.ingramcontent.com/pod-product-compliance
Lightning Source LLC
Chambersburg PA
CBHW070252230526
45470CB00002B/575